NEW HORIZON OF MISSION

LIFE AND CONTRIBUTION OF
REV. DR. BOBBY CHELLAPPAN

Blessy Bobby

Chennai • Bangalore

CLEVER FOX PUBLISHING
Chennai, India

Published by CLEVER FOX PUBLISHING 2024
Copyright © Blessy Bobby 2024

All Rights Reserved.
ISBN: 978-93-56486-82-9

This book has been published with all reasonable efforts taken to make the material error-free after the consent of the author. No part of this book shall be used, reproduced in any manner whatsoever without written permission from the author, except in the case of brief quotations embodied in critical articles and reviews.

The Author of this book is solely responsible and liable for its content including but not limited to the views, representations, descriptions, statements, information, opinions and references ["Content"]. The Content of this book shall not constitute or be construed or deemed to reflect the opinion or expression of the Publisher or Editor. Neither the Publisher nor Editor endorse or approve the Content of this book or guarantee the reliability, accuracy or completeness of the Content published herein and do not make any representations or warranties of any kind, express or implied, including but not limited to the implied warranties of merchantability, fitness for a particular purpose. The Publisher and Editor shall not be liable whatsoever for any errors, omissions, whether such errors or omissions result from negligence, accident, or any other cause or claims for loss or damages of any kind, including without limitation, indirect or consequential loss or damage arising out of use, inability to use, or about the reliability, accuracy or sufficiency of the information contained in this book.

CONTENTS

1. Family 1
2. Friends 48
3. Church Acquaintances 56
4. Associates 82
5. Reflections 87

FAMILY

Biographical Sketch

My memories of my husband….

Pastor Bobby's birth and coming to know Jesus!

Pastor Bobby was born in Agra where mummy, my mother-in-law, was working as a staff nurse then. My mother-in-law's mother raised him in Kerala till he was 3 years old.

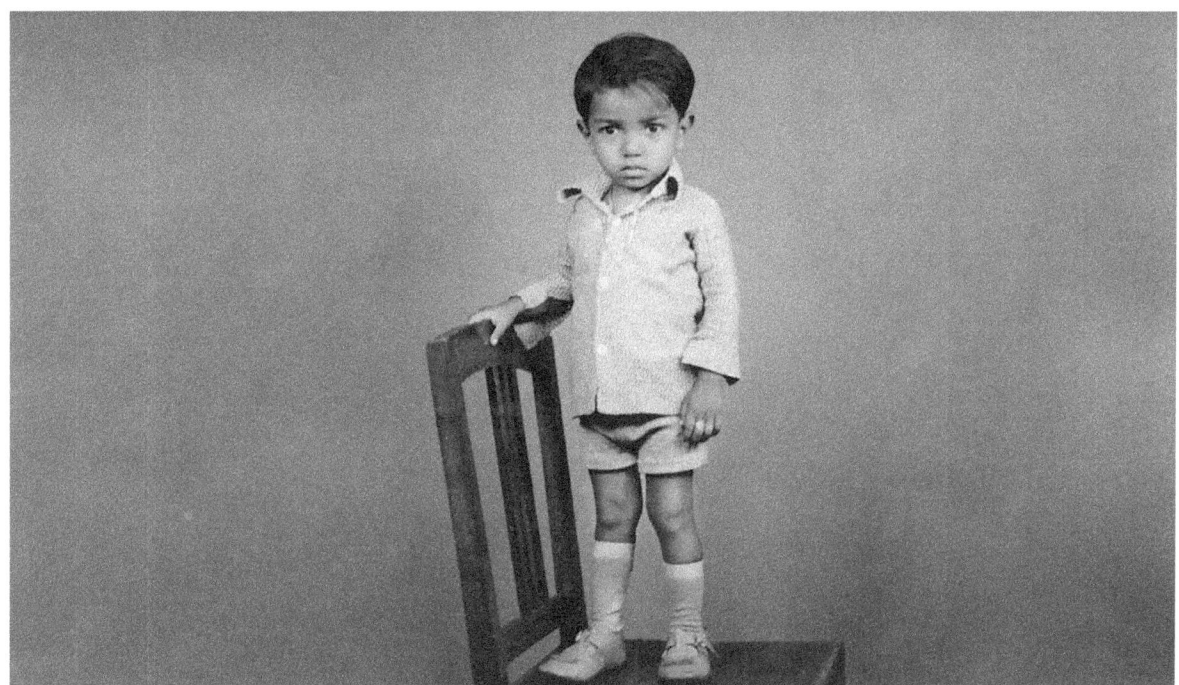

Ps. Bobby as a young boy.

He was then brought to Delhi and grew up under his parents' love and care.

He studied in a private school and was a good student as well as an excellent basketball player, who even played in a state-level competition.

He is from a Hindu family and came to know the Lord Jesus Christ during his school days. During that time, one of his father's brothers was sick in Kerala and they had brought him to Delhi for treatment since my mother-in-law was working at All India Institute of Medical Sciences (AIIMS) as a staff nurse at that time. They tried all kinds of treatment, but the doctors were unable to diagnose his condition. He used to get very violent at times, hitting people, and had to be tied up to be restrained. Bobby and his parents had a tough time during that time with him in their small house in Ayurvigyan Nagar Medical Quarters.

They tried all sorts of treatments but to no avail. Daddy had just joined a new job at NHPC and couldn't go to work because he had to take care of his brother, who listened only to him. They were like any typical Hindu family that believed in conducting daily prayers and rituals and had a place for deities to whom they offered prayers. All the religious holy books were placed there including the Bhagwat Gita, Quran, and a copy of the New Testament Bible.

My father-in-law knew about Jesus and used to attend Church when he was at Bangalore for his Air Force training. One day, Daddy was sitting in a chair just next to his brother who was lying on the bed, and he happened to sigh and called out the name 'Jesus!' Suddenly, his brother got up and pointing towards Daddy said, "Not that name". Daddy was amused as to why he said that. So, he took the Bhagwat Gita that was kept in the Pooja area and gave it to his brother. He took the book and embraced it. Then, Daddy took the Bible and gave it to him, and he flung it out.

Daddy then knew that his brother needed prayers more than any treatment. Daddy went looking for a Church nearby and that was when someone mentioned to him about a Church near their house in Green Park where they could get him prayed over. So, he went to Green Park as advised, and met Dr. Paul Pillai, who was the priest of that church. Seeing Daddy's condition, he asked him to bring his sick brother and leave him at their place for prayer till he got healed. Daddy went home, brought his brother and left him with the believers in that Church who were praying in a hall.

Dr. Paul Pillai assured him that they would continue to pray till he was healed, and that Daddy could go home in peace. Daddy left his brother there with them and went home. And Dr. Paul Pillai and the believers of that Church continued to pray for Daddy's brother. Around midnight, a demonic spirit manifested in Daddy's brother which said that it was there to kill him. Pillai Uncle along with the believers prayed and Uncle rebuked that spirit in the name of Jesus and commanded it to leave his body. Immediately, Daddy's brother fell down unconscious for some time and the evil spirit left him. When he woke up after a few minutes, he was totally healed and normal. That is how Bobby and his parents came to know about the power of Jesus and accepted him as their Lord and Savior.

They took water baptism and joined Dr. Paul Pillai's church. Bobby started attending Sunday School in that Church, where children were taught the Word of God. He was filled with a passion since then to learn more about Jesus and the Bible. He would spend time reading and studying the Word of God and told me later that Daddy and he wouldn't miss any Bible study or meetings in their church. He said he always sat in the front row, eager to learn and would diligently take down notes, go back home and study them repeatedly.

He would share about the love of Jesus to his friends and that's how his next-door neighborhood friend Bro. Jiju got saved.

Ps. Bobby with his friend

When he was alone at home, he said he would stand in front of the mirror and preach what he had learned, hoping to be a preacher someday. Later as he grew up, this passion in him for the Word of God kept increasing.

In those days, if there was any convention or crusade in the city, he would eagerly attend that meeting and have anointed men of God lay hands upon him and pray and pass on the mantle of anointing. He did his vocational training in tourism after his graduation in commerce. He took up a part-time job along with his vocational training and had also started ministering with Daddy in their newly started Church in Malviya Nagar.

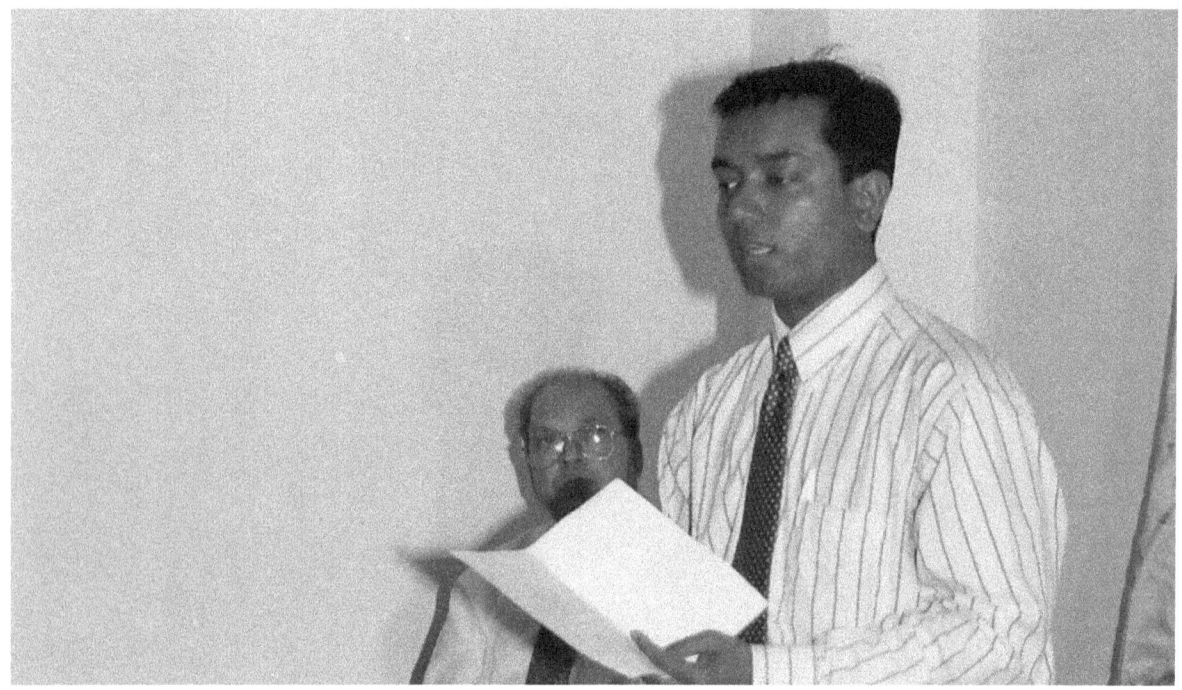

Early days in ministry, with Rev. Dr. Paul Pillai in the newly started church at Malviya Nagar.

In 1999, Daddy fell sick, and the responsibility of the Church fell on Bobby's shoulders. He, being young and inexperienced, looked up at the Lord for guidance. While Daddy was in the hospital for almost 6 months, Bobby would come back home from work and would spend hours praying at night, reading the Bible and books written by famous Christian authors like Benny Hinn, Reinhard Bonnke, and so on.

The Lord started anointing him and he would attend prayer meetings at night at Pastor K R Abraham's Church at Devli. He would go there straight from work at night, pray from 10 pm to 2 am, sleep there, wake up at 6 am, get ready and go to work the next day. This went on for months till God started using him mightily for His glory.

Meanwhile, Daddy had 2 surgeries – a below knee and then an above knee amputation due to diabetic gangrene. Being in God's presence with brothers and sisters in Christ during that time helped Bobby cope with the adverse situation that he faced at home.

My family coming to know about Jesus:

I am also from a Hindu family and my mother's friend, who is a Christian, gave me a Christian name – Blessy – when I was born. As we read in the Bible in Psalms 139:13-17, Isaiah 44:24, Jeremiah 1:5, God knows us even before we are born or even before we are formed in the womb of our mother. My father's name is Krishnan and my mother's name is Radha, which are names of Hindu gods.

When I was five years old, my father was diagnosed with liver cirrhosis and kidney failure. Doctors said that he would not live for more than 7 days. My mother got the report and was so sad that she planned to commit suicide by jumping in front of a running train on her way back home. With the reports in her hand, as she was coming to the railway station, she heard a voice behind her saying 'Jesus heals the sick'. She turned to see who it was, but there was no one there. Such peace came upon her that all her sadness and gloom were gone. She found a new ray of hope. She came back home and found a 'New Testament Bible' that her Christian friend had given her a long time ago, but she never read it. She opened it and read all the miracles that Jesus did. Faith arose in her heart that Jesus could heal my father. That night there was a bright light in our house, and she heard a voice again saying 'Daughter, you believe in me, and I will heal you.'

In the morning, she told my father about the report and her experiences. There was an aunty in our neighborhood who believed in Jesus. My mother shared her experiences with her. As it was a Sunday morning, and she was going to Church, she invited my mother to come to church. My mother took me along to church. For the first time, we heard that 'Jesus is not the God of Christians' and that 'He is the Savior of all mankind and our healer too. By his suffering on the cross, he paid the price for the sins of all mankind and by His stripes, we are healed, if we believe in His sacrifice for us.'

My mother believed that Jesus could save her husband. The pastor of that Church and some believers came home and shared about 'Jesus' with my father. They fasted and prayed for my father for 3 days and on the 7th day, he went for his check-up and all his reports were normal. God miraculously healed my father, who is still alive and pastoring 2 churches in Mumbai by God's grace.

Since then, I started attending Church and Sunday school regularly. I accepted the Lord as my Savior and was filled with the Holy Spirit when I was 9 years old. When I was 15, I took water baptism and since then had a great passion for reading the Word of God and books by Christian authors that my mother bought from stalls during prayer conventions held in Mumbai. After completing my 12th standard, I went to Vellore to study B. Sc Nursing at CMC Vellore in 1996.

Being away from home, missing my parents and sisters back home, saw me through a time of coming closer to the Lord than before. God also miraculously healed me of mitral valve prolapse while I was in my 2nd year when medication didn't work; by believing the Word of God that says in Isaiah 53:5, and 1 Peter 2:24 that by the stripes of Jesus, I am healed. This deepened my faith in the Lord and the Power of His Word.

Our marriage

It was in 2001 that God brought us together. Bobby was from Delhi, and I am from Mumbai. Neither of us nor our families had any contacts in either of these places. I first met Pastor Bobby after my parents received his visiting card after a prayer meeting held in our house in Mumbai.

A pastor, who met Bobby in one of the meetings in Delhi, handed over that card to my father and asked him to call Bobby when my father told him that they were seeking a suitable match for me. I was doing my internship at CMC Vellore at that time after having completed my B.Sc. in Nursing. When I came home that year, my father told me about this proposal and showed me Pastor Bobby's photograph that his father had sent when he contacted him. I was quite impressed by this young man whom I saw in the photograph and my youngest sister, Bincy, approved of the proposal at first sight. In the Indian culture, in an arranged marriage, first it is the boy who visits the girl along with his family. But since Bobby's father had an amputated leg due to gangrene and found it difficult to travel, he asked my father if we could come over to Delhi to visit them as he wished to see me.

My father planned our visit to Delhi accordingly and we came to meet Bobby and his parents along with one of my maternal uncles. We met briefly for a few minutes in Bobby's home in the presence of his parents and some relatives. Since we both approved of the proposal, our families planned the engagement the very next day and we were married two months later in May 2001.

Wedding at Delhi

At the wedding reception at Mumbai

Ps 1:1-3 says-

¹Blessed is the one

who does not walk in step with the wicked

or stand in the way that sinners take

or sit in the company of mockers,

² but whose delight is in the law of the Lord,

and who meditates on his law day and night.

³ That person is like a tree planted by streams of water,

which yields its fruit in season

and whose leaf does not wither—

whatever they do prospers.

That has been my husband's life. He was a God-fearing man and a man of prayer. The day we got married I remember going to the hotel room after our wedding at the Connaught Palace. We knelt on the carpet in the room, holding our hands together and Bobby prayed the most beautiful prayer I have ever heard, surrendering our lives to God. Since that day, we often woke up every morning and spent time in God's presence, praising and worshipping God, reading, and meditating the Word of God, and praying in tongues for God's blessings upon our family, loved ones, Church, nation, and the nations, before we went about our work.

Praying together

At a wedding in Delhi

Ps. Bobby ministering at church

Visit to Taj Mahal

In Hongkong, enjoying a foot massage.

Ps. Bobby at his workplace with colleagues

Enjoying with friends

Bobby was then working as a travel consultant with Cox and Kings, and I got my bond of 2 years shifted to St. Stephen's hospital, Delhi from CMC, Vellore where I worked as a staff nurse in the Surgical ICU. For the next 2 years, we were busy with our work and taking care of the small Church that God helped my Father-in-law, Pastor V. N. Chellappan to start in 1999. There was also a small gathering every Sunday evening at a place called Mayur Vihar.

Birth of our first son

In 2003, our son Samuel was born. While I was 3 months pregnant, we were attending a fasting prayer one day at one of our believer's houses. A guest Pastor had come over to minister that day. We had never met before. After the meeting, he called Bobby and said that God will give us a son and he will be like Samuel, the prophet mentioned in the Bible. So, when our son was born, we named him Samuel.

Just before Samuel was born, a month before my delivery was due, Bobby had a stroke while at his workplace one evening. I was at my home in Mumbai a month before that, as we had planned to have the baby there at my parent's request. Bobby was in the ICU for a week then, recovering from a brain hemorrhage and paralysis of the right side of his body. By God's grace, he recovered miraculously and was able to regain strength within a few weeks, though it took him almost 6 months to recover completely. Soon after his discharge from the hospital, I went into an early labor one Sunday morning on the 8th of June 2003. I had wished to have the baby on Sunday and was glad when my labor pain started early morning on Sunday.

I got ready for Church as usual, but the pain progressed leading me to the labor room and Samuel was born by around 4 pm that day. Since Bobby was still recovering, he couldn't make it during the delivery. But God was by my side throughout that time. A sister from Church told me to keep calling on Jesus when I got the labor pain, and I did just that.

Around 3:30 pm, lying on that bed in the labor room, beside a glass sliding door, I was in severe pain. Three nurses stood at the end of the bed, talking, and suddenly I noticed a rainbow appear behind a rock on that glass door. And saw Jesus standing smiling at me with a baby in His arms. The baby had a crown on his head and wore a purple dress. I pinched myself to check if I was dreaming because I was wide awake and was wondering if the nurses at my foot end of the bed could also see what I was seeing.

Within a few minutes, I could bear the pain no longer and I kept calling the Lord saying- 'Jesus', 'Jesus!' in my mind, till they sedated me just before delivering Samuel. Just before I heard the baby's first cry, I saw 2 angels. They were dressed in white like they were from ancient times. They held out a baby wrapped in white clothes and handed over the baby to me. At that moment, Samuel was born; I heard the first cry, after which I blacked out and remained unconscious for about an hour.

Bobby came to visit his first-born as soon as he could, within a week. The joy of holding his first-born son knew no bounds as we praised God together for this precious gift that He had given us and for healing Bobby so miraculously.

Ps. Bobby with his new-born son Samuel

Family

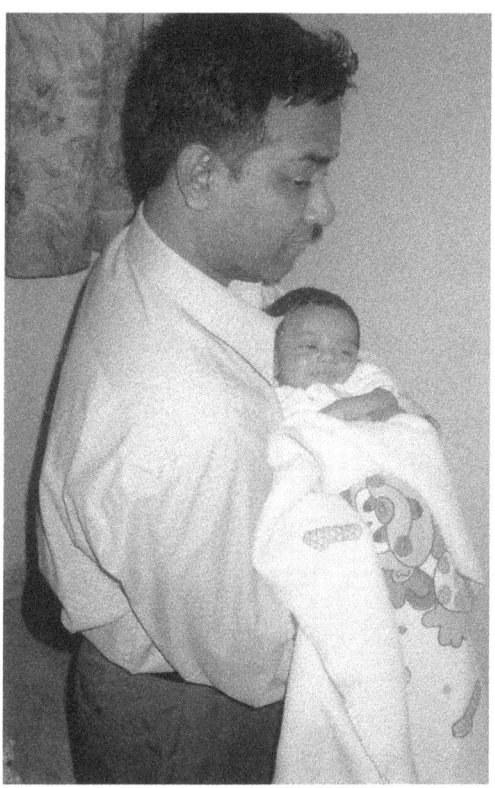

Father-son moments!

We returned to Delhi with our new-born child who, being the first-born, brought such joy to both our families.

Playtime with Samuel

Samuel started growing up seeing his father pastoring the church and at a very young age became actively involved in church activities. Even while he was a baby in my womb towards the later months, I would read out the Bible loudly to him daily, especially from the book of Samuel.

Samuel reciting Psalms 23 at church

02122012037.mp4

Within 6 months of recovering completely, from 2001-2003 Bobby got busy with work. Shouldering the responsibility of being a new father as well as work and ministry.

Ps. Bobby at a restaurant in Shimla

God's grace upon our life kept increasing as we saw the Lord building His Church in the city. During my early days in Delhi, there were few churches, and every Church had very few people. But, during that time, people were hungry for God. There were many prayer meetings in the city, and Bobby, and I joined every meeting possible- fasting prayers, night prayers, combined Church fellowships, with our new-born baby. It was during this time that God started filling us with a fresh passion to serve Him. My younger sister Bindu and her husband

Febin also shifted to Delhi during this time. They stayed in the same colony as us and were a great support to us in the ministry.

Birth of our daughter

In 2005, we shifted to a new place in South Delhi as the place we were staying in was overpopulated and congested. My father-in-law bought a small piece of land in another part of South Delhi called Chattarpur, and we shifted there in September. Just 5 days later, God blessed us with our baby girl, Sarah.

Ps. Bobby with daughter Sarah

Sarah reciting a story in Hindi at church.

03062011030.mp4

She also grew up loving the Lord from her early days seeing her parents and grandparents serve the Lord. She developed a great passion for worshipping the Lord. She had developed an eye condition when she was about 3 years old that the Lord healed when she believed and prayed with faith. This experience deepened her faith in the Lord and has led her to share her testimony with others right from her childhood days.

Daddy and Mummy started a small fellowship at home and people from the neighborhood started joining in. Daddy bought a small Church Hall for us in Malviya Nagar, where Bobby and I continued to minister. Bobby was also busy with work as he took up a new job with the Birla's as the National Head of their travel company in Delhi. Two months after Sarah was born, I was preparing to take my NCLEX exams as I had cleared my CGFNS and was preparing to go to the United States as a staff nurse.

My embassy interview date was in October 2006. But in April 2006, a month before my NCLEX exams, Bobby had a sudden heart attack. He had to undergo an angioplasty and they had to put in a stent to open his artery that was 90% blocked. It took a week for him to come out of that critical condition from the ICU.

As they were taking him into the surgical theatre for angioplasty, Bobby wanted to tell me that if he died during the surgery, not to bury him as his time had not yet come. But there were so many people around him that he couldn't convey this message to me then; he later told me this. And as they were taking him into the operation theatre for surgery, my world nearly crashed.

People around me were all crying, but suddenly, an unusual peace overtook me. Standing there outside the operation theatre, I heard a voice, as someone had just switched on a tape recorder loudly in my mind; someone telling me- "Surely, goodness and mercy shall follow me all the days of my life and I will dwell in the house of the Lord forever." This verse from a psalm in the Bible played continuously in my mind repeatedly for the next 24 hours till Bobby stabilized after surgery. And I knew that God was in control of our situation and that Bobby would get better.

Bobby was discharged from the hospital a week later, but for the next 6 months it was like facing death every single day. Even as I took him to the bathroom each day, he would have severe palpitations and I feared if I could get him back to the bed, alive. The doctor had advised us that he should slowly start moving around. God was gracious to us and within 6 months, Bobby recovered. Though he was on medication and diet control, he was able to function normally.

Ministering passionately

Ps. Bobby with family at IGI Airport Delhi, before going to Nigeria for 'Rupantar' movie editing

Our plans Vs. God's plan

Meanwhile, in August 2006, the US government passed a retrogression saying that they would not be recruiting foreign nurses. With Bobby's health condition, this was another blow to us. All our plans were just shattered. But God had a different plan. I started working part-time with Max Health staff as an NCLEX trainer 2 months after Sarah was born.

When Bobby fell ill, hearing about Bobby's condition and the retrogression scene, the Principal of Max Health staff called to ask me if I could work for them as a full-time trainer. This was the first time that they were offering a student that kind of an offer and at a salary more than all the other staff since I had cleared my NCLEX. But I knew this was God's favor upon our life. In October one of my teachers from Max Health Staff called to ask if I would like to join a Multinational company in Gurgaon that was planning to start a medical department. She said they were offering me a pay more than what I would have earned in the US, and I could hardly believe it. Bobby and I had been praying and we knew that it was God's favor upon us again and I accepted the offer.

Since it was a well-paying job, I asked a teacher of mine from Max Health Staff and 2 students as well to join this company along with me. They too agreed. We got trained for a month for a process called 'Utilization Management' which was supposed to be night shifts, but after training, the process didn't turn up. However, our

Employer didn't let us go and we continued to be part of that company for the next few years. For almost nine months, we were paid without having to do any work and I knew that this was again God helping me cope with my situation.

Bobby was at home, taking care of his health and the kids as well. Sarah was still a baby and needed care and God provided us with a maid who stayed with us and helped take care of her. She also helped my mother-in-law with household work while I was away at work. We lived in a joint family then, with my brother-in-law, Robby, and sister-in-law, Sarika, who were also very supportive of us.

Growth of the Church

During this time, God's favor came upon the Church as well as we saw the Church grow. We started having regular cell meetings in various places in people's houses. I would come back from work each day to join Bobby in the evenings for these meetings.

Serving together

God started moving miraculously. People started getting saved by the power of the gospel and we had about 40 baptisms in 2007. Slowly more people started getting saved as God led us strategically to pray, plan and implement prayer and evangelism movements across the city. Uncle Singsit, an elder from the city of Delhi, who had great burden for the city, called Bobby to lead a prayer movement 24*7 involving all the churches in Delhi from 2007-10. It was a great time of revival in Delhi then, when he along with a few other pastors from the city set out to work, associating and networking with various Pastors and leaders in the city dividing the area into north, south, east, and west zones, and mobilizing prayer.

Praying as a church at Apostolic Faith Church, Malviya Nagar

At a wedding ceremony with a brother from church

Teams from different churches would gather at one Church for 24 hours and worship and pray for the city and nation. Prayer drives were also conducted in and around the city and we would meet regularly at strategic locations with Pastors and leaders and pray for a breakthrough. Soon, churches started growing, people started coming in and getting saved like never before.

At Bless India festival, Talkatora Stadium, Delhi

Today, by God's grace, there are over 5000 growing churches in Delhi. God also opened doors for Bobby to pursue his higher studies and get a Doctorate in Theology and for me to do my post-graduation in business management and to get a promotion to be a Healthcare Management Consultant at work. I also saw the favor of God at my workplace as our company began to prosper and be profitable.

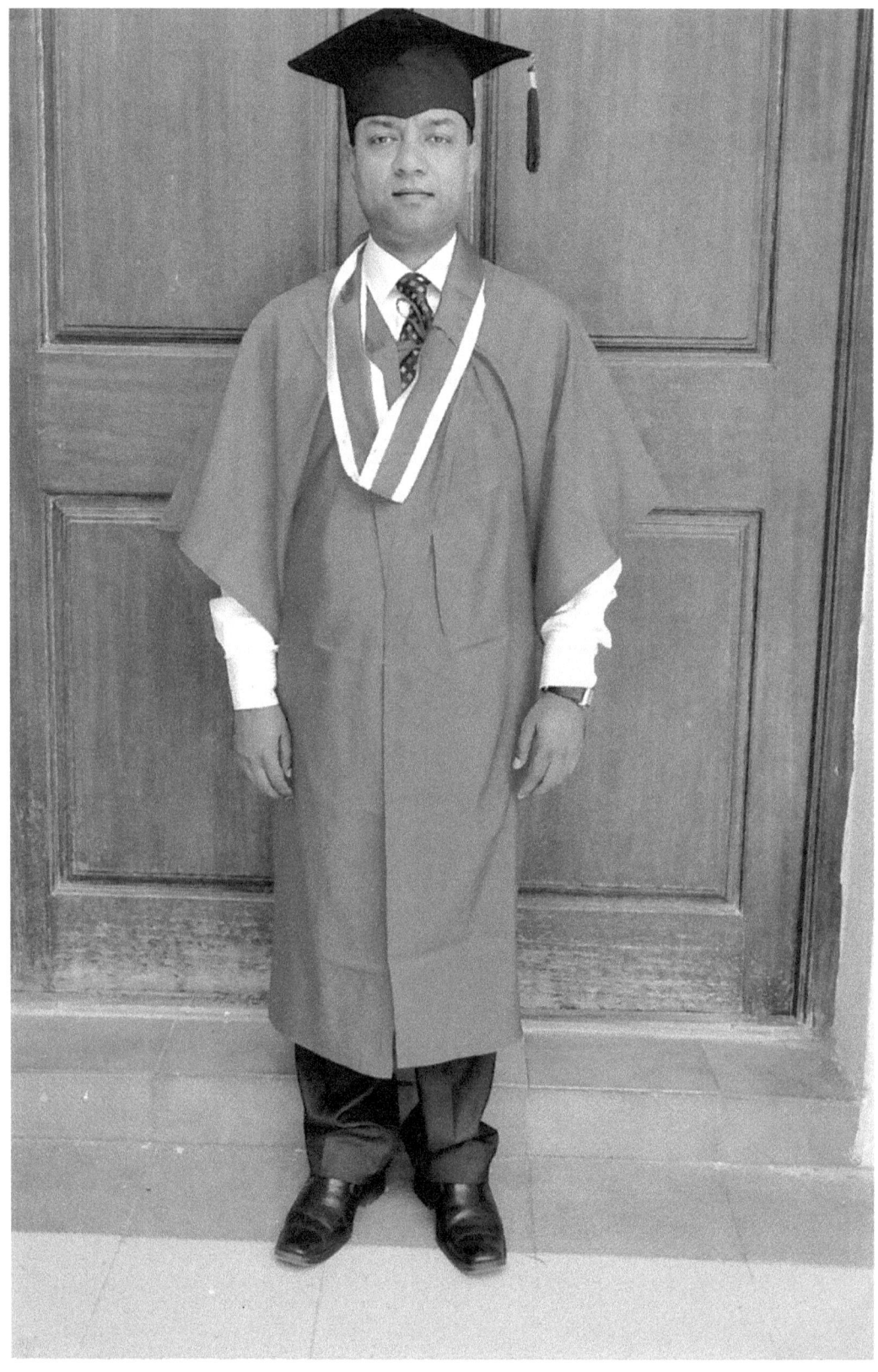

Dr. Bobby on completing his Doctorate in Theology from the University of Jerusalem, Chennai

Relaxing at a restaurant

At Himachal, on vacation

God also opened doors for us in the media to preach the Word of God on FETV which reached out to about 120 countries. So, for a year from 2009-10, we spent our weekends recording messages, worship songs, short skits and other programs involving various churches around the city. We received good feedback and people were getting saved, touched, and transformed worldwide. We were excited about what God was doing in and through our lives.

25122010051.mp4

Choreography by the children at church during Christmas

God's call!

And then one day we were at a summer retreat in Dehradun with Pastor KR Abraham and Pastor Chandy Varghese and their families and youth group from our churches, God spoke to me about quitting my job and joining Bobby in full-time ministry. I was unprepared for this, but the conviction was so strong and when God confirmed it to Bobby as well during this time, we decided to give up my job and obey God's call.

Holding on to God's promises and each other

There was great opposition and persecution that we faced soon after from our family who thought we had gone crazy. But God stood strong on our behalf and led us through miraculously each day. Until then, we had read from the Bible about the God of Abraham, Isaac, and Jacob. But since then, we started learning that He is our God too as we walked by faith each day.

Serving God joyfully!

We started looking up to God for all our needs and experienced His love and provision in supernatural ways. It deepened our relationship with God more than ever before as we learned to trust Him every step of the way. Meanwhile, God provided Bobby with opportunities to teach in the Grace Bible College.

Ministering at church

Baptising a sister in Ludhiana, Punjab

People started inviting us to various churches in the city, as well as around North India to minister from the Word of God. We saw the mighty hand of God upon our lives as we saw God touching and transforming lives, mighty miracles happened before our very eyes as we ministered and people from all walks of life were delivered from sin, sickness, and bondages. Bobby would travel more as I needed to be at home for the kids. The apostolic mandate to fulfil the great commission as in Mathew 28:18-20 and Acts 1:8 took over our lives.

Visit to Bible Museum, US

Happy to be together as a family

Ministry life

And we saw God building our church, raising many pastors and leaders whom God started using to plant more churches in the city and a few states of North India like Bihar, Chhattisgarh, Haryana etc. God filled us with such a passion to serve Him that we would be back home past midnight most days, spending time in prayer with our people in their homes, training and equipping them in the Word, counseling and mentoring them. It was also during this time in 2011 that God connected us to Dr. John Joseph who facilitated the start-up of a Bible training module at our Church in association with Life Christian University, USA to train and equip our people in the Word of God. This program which was started as a certificate 1-year course was such a blessing and it now has B. Th. and M.Th. degree programs as well. Many of our people are blessed by this course and being raised with a strong foundation in the Word of God as leaders in God's kingdom.

2012-16, we were fully focused on our ministry. The Church grew and flourished. In May 2013 , my father-in-law, who had been bedridden for a long time due to illness, went home to be with the Lord. My mother-in-law was sick during his last days and within 6 months she had a paralytic attack and was bedridden for the next 5 years until she went home to be with the Lord in June 2018.

A turning point- Bible translation!

In 2016, as we were praying, one day the Lord told Bobby that He was going to move him into something higher. We wondered what it was and that's when Cmdr. Thomas Mathew called up to ask him if he could head their Bible Translation Department. As we prayed about it, the Lord reminded us of a prophecy that a man of God named Jeremy Sunder Raj had made concerning this a few years ago while we were at a meeting.

There was this fasting prayer going on in Pastor Abraham's Church at Masih Ghar and as Pastor Jeremy was preaching, he suddenly called Bobby to the front from amongst the crowd and started prophesying that he would be like the great missionary William Carey in this generation, who translated the Bible into many Indian languages. He did mention a few details about his work and asked two people to write it down and hand it over to Bobby. I still have those notes written on small sheets of paper that those two people faithfully noted down. He, then, called me to the front and told me that I needed to stand with him through this work, prayed over both of us and blessed us along with the congregation.

We were also reminded of what God had spoken to him personally a few days ago and so being fully convinced, he decided to take up the work that Cmdr. Thomas Mathew offered him. There were just a handful of employees when Bobby took up the work and this was something that he had no training for. But God was with him and endowed him with the anointing, wisdom, and skills that he needed to bring this work to fruition.

Slowly, the work began to progress from revising the old Bible text into 12 major Indian languages and then to some minority languages in which there was no Bible yet. God blessed the work and slowly they set up a studio to do the audio recording of the Bibles that were getting translated and to get worship songs translated into Indian languages, especially minority languages. Meanwhile, there were other projects coming in for translating theological literature and Bible stories into Indian languages and to get them into audio and video format. Thereby, the team grew and today we are about 100 employees working to get the work done that the Lord started in us.

It was in 2018 April, that Bobby asked me if I could do the audio recording for the Indian Revised Version of the Hindi Bible in the newly set up studio. From 2016-18 was a tough time for me as Bobby was majorly involved with his work responsibilities and travel to meet Bishops, Pastors, and Church leaders of various Indian states to get their approval for the community check processes that were set up to get the Bibles through an authentic accuracy review before getting it out to the public.

Shouldering the Church responsibility and taking care of Mummy who was bedridden due to paralysis as well as managing home kept me on my toes during those days. While I took up the audio work, we handed over the Church responsibility to an assistant pastor who beautifully managed it with his family till a few months ago when they left to start a new church. God also provided us with a maid to help take care of mummy during her last 3 months as well as the of the kids while we were away at work. This was a huge help that helped us find a couple of hours before bedtime to spend with ministry responsibilities and kids' studies.

From 2018 onwards, the Bible translation work started to blossom. New projects started coming in and the work grew and flourished. With the guidance and supervision of our leaders- Dr. Babu Abraham and Cmdr. Thomas Mathew different departments were set up involving the Translation department, the Software Department, the Print on Demand Department, The Audio Department, and our Administration Department.

With colleagues at the office picnic

We met every morning in the conference hall for a time of prayer and devotion after which we all set to work. Everyone put in their best to make sure the work was done as per our quality requirements and client satisfaction. This period also saw us building up connections with various client organizations. The development of the Vachanonline website and Vachango app was an added milestone. It gave us a good platform to make our resources available for free as creative commons for the use and development of the Church community and unreached people groups. God has been good and faithful all along and led us victoriously through many challenging situations that our staff faced during this time along with their families as they were involved with the work. But each one was determined to go ahead with the work, come what may, and we are grateful to God who kept adding faithful workers to our team.

There are about 750 Indian languages of which only 80 have a full Bible. The task ahead is huge as we go forward with the vision of reaching out to the nations with scripture in all languages by 2033.

Even as Jesus said in Mathew 9:37,38 -[37] "The harvest is plentiful, but the workers are few. [38] Ask the Lord of the harvest, therefore, to send out workers into his harvest field." That's our prayer today, as we seek the Lord to accomplish all that is in His heart for us in this generation. Bobby set to work skilfully leading his team with God-given wisdom even as we read about David in the Bible, in Psalms 78:70-72-

[70] He chose David his servant

and took him from the sheep pens;

[71] from tending the sheep he brought him

to be the shepherd of his people, Jacob,

of Israel his inheritance.

[72] And David shepherded them with the integrity of heart;

with skillful hands, he led them.

Work and ministry

God also started opening doors for us to reach out to the deaf community in India by enabling Bobby to facilitate the translation of the Bible into the Indian Sign Language (ISL) for the first time in India.

This work was picking up momentum amongst others and Bobby was extremely busy working throughout the lockdown time often from 7 am to late into the night without any rest. Anytime people approached him for meetings online or offline, he would always be ready. This was the time that the Lord opened doors for us to minister on social media, i.e., on Facebook and YouTube.

After church

Family

Celebrating 20 years of Apostolic Faith Church with Ps. David Dhillan, Morris Cerullo Ministries

His voice continues to reach out with the gospel on these platforms and I am so grateful to the Lord who made this possible. He was so engrossed in his work that one day I walked into our room to sleep, tired after the day's work, and was shocked to see him ready at his desk in his suit, coat, and tie, and I couldn't help but burst out laughing. He laughed too and said, "I forgot to tell you. I need to preach in a meeting now in London at Pastor Jolly Lazar's- 'Shake the Nation's' meeting online. It's till 1 am." He continued to do his office work as well as minister this way online till he had a sudden heart attack last year on July 14th, 2021.

That day, he ministered in 3 different meetings online. After the last meeting with Pastor KR Abraham's Church online, we had our dinner at around 9:30 pm. That night we talked over dinner and at bedtime, he sat up in bed, unable to lie down due to acidity. The acidity seemed to increase, and I gave him an antacid. When the discomfort persisted, on checking his blood pressure, I was shocked. It was very low, and we rushed him to the hospital. He insisted that we take him to a private hospital near our house. I was hesitant at first knowing that it was a very expensive hospital. But since he insisted, I conceded. Being a wife, over the years, God taught me to trust my husband's decisions to be the best for us. On reaching the hospital, the doctor said that he had a massive heart attack and that the previous stent was also 100 percent blocked. He needed immediate surgery. The doctor was quite apprehensive to do the surgery as it was very risky. But he finally did, and Bobby was shifted to the ICU for monitoring.

Meanwhile, we informed our pastor, a few close relatives, and our directors at work and people started praying for his recovery. Even before admitting him, the hospital informed us that their charges were about 1 lakh a day. Trusting God to come through, I consented. After surgery, Bobby was out of the ventilator within 24 hours and recovering well. Then the doctors planned the second surgery to open the previously blocked stent after 4-5 days.

Meanwhile, Bobby was getting better, happy to see us all and we were so grateful to God for helping him recover. Our Church was continuously praying, and I am grateful to them for organizing those special prayers for Bobby during that time and to our brothers and sisters who prayed, sometimes all through the night. Also grateful to Cmdr. Thomas Mathew our Managing Director and Dr. Babu Abraham and our colleagues who continuously offered their prayerful support and encouraging visits.

I am also grateful to Light the World Missions Director-Rev. Dr. Joseph Mathew, Pastor Ranjit Panicker and their prayer team and The National prayer team headed by Pastor Libish Abraham for continuously praying and conducting special prayers for Bobby's speedy recovery. By God's grace and everyone's prayers, the second surgery was also successful. But that night I had a dream, and I saw that I went to visit Bobby at the hospital and his bed was empty. I shared this with my pastor and my family, but none of them said anything.

Soon after, Bobby acquired a hospital infection that affected his blood and his condition started deteriorating. I remember the doctor's team, along with the Medical Superintendent, calling us for a meeting after a week to tell us that they had no hope of his survival and to inform our family, relatives, and friends of his prognosis.

Though dejected by the doctor's report, we still hoped for a miracle and the Church was interceding for us. Meanwhile, I informed my parents and close relatives of the doctor's report and my parents who were in Canada at that time came down with my sister Bincy and her family to visit Bobby and to be with us during this time.

Also, Bro. Sudhir from our Church came over with his wife Mamta and the children. Mamta stayed home with the children for over 2 weeks and was a great help and support while I was in the hospital with Bobby. We had a few savings that we had kept for migrating to Florida, USA as Bobby was due to join our client organization Unfolding Word in August to take on the global Bible translation work along with Dr. David Reeves and his team. I was paying the hospital bills with that money.

God's divine intervention

One day, while I was at the hospital, with just enough money to pay the bills for the next 2 days, I got a call. It was from Rev. Minny Lal, the Indian Co-ordinator and Associate Minister of Morris Cerullo Ministries. She had been associated with us since 2007 and had been a spiritual mother to Bobby and me since then. A woman of great faith, she was a great source of encouragement to Bobby and me during those initial years of our faith walk with the Lord when we both quit our secular jobs to serve the Lord.

That day, she enquired about Bobby's health and told me that she was not feeling any peace and release in her spirit as she prayed for Bobby's healing. Then she asked me how I was managing the bills as she said super rich people also wouldn't be able to afford that hospital's bills. I said, "God has provided so far, and I trust him to do that in future as well." She then prayed a very beautiful prayer that God answered and left me, and many others awe-struck at the Lord's doing. She prayed that God who was 'Jehovah Jireh' our Provider as the Bible says, would provide for the hospital expenses and that I would have enough left over to sow in God's Kingdom after that.

That very night, I received a Facebook notification and was shocked to see that my pastor, my sister Bincy, and brother-in-law Jobby had started a Milaap fund to raise funds for Bobby's treatment. The next day onwards, it was as if heavens opened to intervene. People from across the globe started connecting with us- praying, interceding and supporting us. I was deeply touched by the love, prayers, and support of people worldwide, especially of some whom I didn't even know.

Throughout those 40 days in the hospital, as I waited on Bobby, I experienced the Lord's presence every moment as a friend with friend. He never left me even for a moment. I felt angelic assistance when I traveled to and from the hospital and even now it continues to be so. Every time, I joined those prayers with my brothers and sisters who were praying, God filled me with supernatural peace, comfort, and encouragement.

Our loved ones, close relatives, and friends, pastors, brothers, and sisters from the Church and the city as well as our colleagues kept visiting us at the hospital. Many of them couldn't even see Bobby as he was in the ICU, but they kept coming to visit and encourage me throughout our stay at the hospital. I am so grateful to God for such love and loving and caring brothers and sisters that God has blessed us with. May God richly bless and reward each one of them; that is my prayer.

All throughout the hospitalization, except for a few days after surgery when Bobby was on the ventilator, the doctors were surprised that he was conscious, oriented, and communicating well. He was very happy to see his visitors and would meet them joyfully. When I would meet him, he would enquire about our children and was very happy whenever Sam and Sarah visited him.

He was concerned about his work even then and would often talk about official meetings and enquire about our Director. Being in the hospital for so long, took a toll on his health and immunity. He got some hospital-acquired infections and had to be started on dialysis. Till 11 pm on the 25th of August, he was conscious and communicating with the staff on duty despite his tracheostomy. But on 26th August 2021 at 3:48 am, he breathed his last breath here on earth and entered his heavenly abode to be with His Master forever. His testimony would be like Apostle Paul says in 2 Timothy 4:7, 8- "⁷I have fought the good fight, I have finished the race, I have kept the faith. ⁸ Now there is in store for me the crown of righteousness, which the Lord, the righteous Judge, will award to me on that day—and not only to me, but also to all who have longed for his appearing."

Though we miss him greatly every single day, we have this hope as an anchor to our souls that we will meet him someday beyond the other shore. Was truly blessed to have him as my husband and I am so grateful to God for leading us through this journey of life in His path that leads to eternity with Him.

I heard a beautiful hymn - "In the sweet, by and by, we shall meet on that beautiful shore…."; play twice in my mind aloud, as Bobby's heart rate dropped in the ICU and I was in the waiting area. That opened my insight into the spiritual realm where the Word of God say's about a husband and wife's relationship that- "They two shall be one flesh (Gen 2:24, Mark 10:8,9 and Ephesians 5:31). That song has given me much hope ever since that we will meet again on that beautiful shore.

If you have lost a loved one or going through some grief or trouble in your life, I want to encourage you to come to the Lord Jesus Christ, invite Him into your heart as your Lord and Savior and let Him carry you through life's journey victoriously even as He has been carrying me, our children, our church and ministry and work beautifully even as Bobby rests in the arms of our Lord.

In the sweet, by and by, we shall meet on that beautiful shore….

Much love,

Blessy Bobby

Wife

Dad left behind a Legacy to carry on….

My Daddy was a person who was ever ready for God's work all the time. In the past years, I saw how dedicated he was towards God's work. Whenever I went to him, he always taught me to follow God's ways every single day.

He used to be in meetings for hours- sitting in a chair from morning, preaching, teaching, and training. He used to start his day by waking up at 5 in the morning and praying. Then at 7, he will be in a meeting till 9. From 10 am till afternoon he will again be in a meeting and the evening. He used to be up until late at night and that showed me how passionate he was for God's work. He kept his plans and dreams aside and did what God told him to do. During challenging times, he was always an anchor and guided me by encouraging me that I could do it and do it much better.

He was a person who followed God's heart and had a strong conviction about what he believed in. I remember he used to say this- "No matter what happens, no matter what situation you are in and no matter how strong you think the devil is, remember to trust in God as He is our only Savior." Romans 14:8 says- If we live, we live to the Lord; and if we die, we die to the Lord. So, whether we live or die, we belong to the Lord. This verse has always stayed with me because Dad lived each day like that. Every day and night he used to speak God's Word to everyone. People used to call up late at night sometimes for prayer. I wondered how people even 80 years old called him 'bhaiya' which means 'brother' till I saw that he was like a brother to them in so many life situations.

Daddy had such courage and was always willing to preach and teach the Word of God and pray for people, be it any time, even at night. He was a person who will always be my role model. And I just want to say- "Daddy, I love you, and I will miss you and I will carry on the legacy that you have left behind".

Samuel Bobby

Son

"Calmness and Positive Vibes of my Dad"

Just want to write a few lines about my Daddy….

My Daddy was a great husband, pastor, and teacher. But above all that he was the best father I could have ever asked for. A father who loved me a lot and was always there for me, my safest place and shelter. He used to call me Kuttu which means 'baby' in Malayalam and always treated me like his princess even as my name 'Sarah' means.

He, for sure, played a very important role in my life and will always hold a very special place in my heart. He had a pure and beautiful heart. He was not just my Dad but also a good friend to me with whom I used to rant my daily nonsense and bicker a lot. He used to be the one to start it by teasingly calling me some weird names that he would pick from anywhere. But he indeed had a very calm nature with positive vibes.

Whenever I was down or feeling low, he would try to cheer me up by cracking some weird lame jokes which unfortunately didn't work but he would laugh at them anyway as he found them funny. Though this is just a small part of the memories that I had with him, I will indeed treasure every moment that we shared for the rest of my life.

I'll always remember all the teachings he gave me as not only a Pastor or Teacher but as an amazing father. During his last days, I didn't get a chance to tell him how much he meant to me and how much I love him. All those unspoken words lay heavy in my heart. But I know that he knew it, and even though unspoken, he said a lot with his eyes.

Today, as I write these words in memory of him, I want to say "Daddy, I love you so much and I will always miss you. You will always be remembered as long as I live, and I will always keep you and your memories safe".

Sarah Bobby

Daughter

A wonderful brother

My dearest and most beloved elder brother Bobby Chellappan was, for some, Reverend Dr. Bobby Chellappan, but for me he was Bobby bhaiya (a word of respect for an elder brother). We both had a fun childhood in a middle-class family, with loving and caring parents. Bobby bhaiya was 5 years older than me, and we grew up together in a colony where all the doctors, nurses and other staff of the All-India Institute of Medical Sciences lived. So, we had lots of friends of all ages living close by. Bobby bhaiya was quite naughty till around the age of 15, after which he turned his focus on spiritual things and became a Sunday School teacher from being a student.

His transformation had his impact on my life too because I always idolized him and wanted to do things the way he did, though I didn't do well following his footsteps. He was hard-working and ambitious. After finishing school, he joined a Tourism graduation program along with working for a travel agency. I would see him wake up at least two or three times a night and go to the airport to pick up clients for his agency. He worked hard, and his hard work paid off well too as he endeavored to work harder and pray and read the Bible whenever he got the time along with his studies.

Bobby bhaiya was a great sportsman. He was into all kinds of sports, athletics, football, tennis, basketball, cricket, and table tennis. He played for the school teams and won many medals and certificates for his performance.

Last year in April 2021, around 3 months before Bobby bhaiya was admitted to Fortis Hospital in New Delhi, I was infected by the Corona Virus which after a couple of days became severe and I couldn't breathe well due to low oxygen level. I needed oxygen support and hospitalization, but there were no beds available in any of the hospitals. Bobby bhaiya tried the whole night trying to find a hospital, then finally he called up a friend of ours whose wife was a nurse in a government hospital. She somehow managed to reserve a bed for me. Bobby bhaiya, along with another brother Shibu, took me to that hospital in an ambulance without worrying that they might catch the virus too. In fact, while at home he would be always around me day and night. Bobby bhaiya managed to help me save my life. The only regret that I have is that I couldn't do much for him when he was admitted to the hospital. During the time I was in the hospital, he was in constant touch with me through WhatsApp. We got so close to each other once again and opened to each other after a long time. Even when I came back from the hospital till the day he was hospitalized, he would frequently come over to my floor to meet me and spend time talking to each other. We had both lost our mom and dad and the worst fear was to lose each other as well. But Almighty God had other plans for us, and I lost the only other person left in my original family. He suffered for almost a month and a half in the hospital, but I know he is at peace now.

Bobby bhaiya was also my counselor and teacher. I used to go to him with all kinds of questions and he would always help me out. Every time I had questions about the Word of God, I would go to him for answers, and he managed to take the time for me and help me out. I cherish all the family time, birthdays, and anniversaries that we spent time together partying and spending time together with the whole family around.

Bobby bhaiya was a trendsetter when it came to his choice of clothes and accessories. He had this way of always being well-dressed for every occasion. We both got separated for a while when I left for South India to do my bachelor's in hotel management. The place I was in was the den of the underworld and illegal gangs; once I saw a man's throat being slit and I was standing next to him, his blood splashed all over my face after which I was not able to sleep for a long time. During my vacations, I came back home and as usual, was trying to sleep beside Bobby bhaiya, but I would keep having nightmares and would wake up frightened. I would never forget what Bobby bhaiya did for me, every time I woke up frightened, I would see Bobby bhaiya sitting up on his knees praying for me all night long. God saw and heard his diligent and persistent prayers and within a couple of days I started to sleep normally, and the nightmares just vanished. He taught me what sacrificial love was all about. In truth, I obeyed and respected him even more than, I did my parents. I could go on and on about our childhood and youth, but I would just end by thanking God for blessing me with an elder brother like him and I endeavor to be as good, loving, and responsible as he was.

Looking forward to being with him in eternity.

Pastor Robby Chellappan

Brother

A loving son

A few words about my beloved son-in-law Rev Dr. Bobby Chellappan-

First, talked with him through tele-conversation when he was the Chief Manager of Cox & Kings Organization. One Pastor Mathew from PMG Church came to me and handed over a visiting Card of Bobby and asked me to contact him because his parents were seeking a suitable life partner for him. According to his advice, I tried his number, but he was on an official tour in Bangkok. After two days, he returned and contacted me on the phone. I informed him about the marriage proposal of my elder daughter Blessy, who had completed her BSc in Nursing at CMC Vellore and was doing her internship there. Immediately he told me, "Uncle I will request my Daddy to contact you in this matter." I learned from his conversation with me that he was very mature, respected his parents, talked politely, and most of all, was a God-fearing man of God. The next day, his father called me, and we discussed the alliance and by the grace of God, the marriage was arranged. Since his father had an amputated leg due to gangrene, Bobby took all the responsibilities and made all the arrangements for the wedding himself. Bobby and Blessy got married on 13th May 2001 at 'Hotel The Connaught ' at Connaught Place New Delhi and the wedding ceremony was solemnized by Late Rev Dr. K. V. Paul Pillai, Founder of Grace Bible Seminary. I came to know that Bobby had fully dedicated his life to the Lord's ministry and his determination for the expansion of the Kingdom of God was commendable. He was so loving and a very caring son to me and my family. In His time, God called him to Eternal Glory. According to the Word of God - 1 Thes. 4:16-17, we will meet him on the other shore and be with the Lord forever.

Pastor M. K. Kutty

Papa (Father-in-law)

Dr. Bobby Chellappan Memoir

Dr. Bobby Chellappan was my loving brother, an amazing colleague, and a dear mentor. Although we were cousins by relation, we were close to each other as brothers, and I have many fond memories of our childhood growing up together. Even as a young teenager, Bobby bhaiya was responsible and wise beyond his years, and I've personally experienced how he loved and tenderly cared for those around him.

I have a vivid memory of one such incident when bhaiya and I met with a bike accident when I was about 9 years old. bhaiya had offered to take me on his bicycle to Church and I had happily joined him. He placed me on the middle bar of his cycle, and we went our way chatting and enjoying the ride. This wasn't unusual for me as I'd been on his bicycle on many occasions. However, on that day, my feet accidentally got caught in between the wheels and we both fell off the bike. Bhaiya quickly responded to my injury, asking me to relax and gently releasing my stuck feet from the wheel. He then placed me back on the cycle and pedaled as fast as he could to the Church to get first aid. I remember him assuring me that everything was fine and that all would be well. He was by my side caring for me till I got my first aid, and my mom came over. I still have a scar on my feet from that incident and it reminds me of my loving and caring brother who always looked out for us.

I saw him grow into an amazing spiritual leader who had a zeal for the kingdom of God and a genuine burden for churches in Northern India. I saw him serve humbly and share the gospel with all around him irrespective of their background, culture, and social status, as he believed that like Jesus, we too are called to be compassionate and loving to others. He worked tirelessly for the work of God's kingdom. Be it an early morning prayer or a full night prayer, he would make time to attend every possible prayer meeting. And I believe this discipline made him the mighty prayer warrior and an anointed servant of God that he was.

It was a privilege for me to serve together with bhaiya at Apostolic Faith Church for many years and later again for the Bible translation work. For almost four years, bhaiya and I commuted together for work every day, traveled together to many places training translators, equipping the leaders, and sharing the vision of Bible translation with many churches of different denominations. Those years spent together with bhaiya were a gift from God and they brought us much closer as friends, brothers, and co-workers of Christ.

When God opened a way for us to relocate to Canada, I never expected to see bhaiya cry and express his love for us the way he did when we had to say goodbye. He was a loving and affectionate brother to me, and I know from many of our conversations how proud he felt being a husband and a father. He was extremely patient, kind, and most importantly, a humble person; a quality that everybody admired. He lived by faith no matter what the circumstances were. He used to encourage me on multiple occasions that when everything fails, our simple faith in God can move mountains.

Bobby bhaiya will be dearly missed, and he is in our thoughts and will always be fondly remembered. His life and teachings will always remain with us. He diligently served the Lord and faithfully completed his race. I will strive each day to follow the faith and teachings of Christ the way he taught us. And I pray that bhaiya's life and his testimony will be a reason for many lives to be changed and many people may know the saving grace of our Lord and Savior Jesus Christ.

Blessings,

Jobby Prasannan,

Cousin

Dr. Bobby Chellappan was my brother-in-law twice related as he had married my eldest sister Blessy 21 years ago in 2001 while I married his cousin brother Jobby 7 years later. Dr. Bobby was Pastor Bobby or Bobby Bhaiya or simply Bobby for many but for my sister Bindu and I, we lovingly called him Jeeju, which means brother-in-law in Hindi. He was the elder brother that we, sisters, never had and so we welcomed him wholeheartedly into the family.

Jeeju loved God and sought God's will above anything else in his life. He was instrumental in my walk with God and my earliest memories of him were the deep encouraging conversations we used to have for hours about the transformative power of Christ and His Holy Spirit. Every time we met, he was always excited to share powerful testimonies of what the Lord had done in the lives of those around him. I remember once when I was singing the song "Wherever He leads I'll go", he turned around and asked me if I truly meant what I sang and I responded with a yes. He lovingly told me that in that case, although there may be hardships, there is no greater joy than serving the Lord and being in His divine will. Since then, Jeeju's presence as an elder brother and spiritual father figure had a deep impact on my life as I grew older.

My favourite memories are the fun times we spent together as one big family sharing meals and having fellowship after a prayer meeting or on special occasions. Jobby and I would sometimes step out for an evening walk and end up visiting and having a second dinner with Jeeju and my sister at their place. Those were some beautiful memories we have as a family to cherish where we freely laughed, teased each other, and simply enjoyed a good time together. When Jobby and I moved to Canada in 2018 with our two children, it broke our hearts to leave our close-knit family in Delhi. But we were blessed and extremely joyful when Jeeju visited us the next year in our new country. That week was extremely special for both Jobby and me, as we spent a week together as a family. It was a joy to see him delightfully experience the boat tour at Niagara Falls. I never imagined that those beautiful fun-filled moments were going to be some of my last memories with my dearest brother. Today, I thank and praise God for Jeeju's life and I celebrate his memories. Jeeju preached about the abundant life and resurrection power of Christ where there is no room for despair. And so, while his death has been a deep loss and an immensely painful shock for all who loved him, we are encouraged by the fact that the fruit of his passionate hard work in God's kingdom continues to impact and change lives.

Bincy Jobby

Sister-in-law

My experience with Bobby

"Men may come, men may go, but their loving memories never fade."

It was way back in 1982 when I had been to Delhi, after completion of my 10th board exam to spend my summer vacation at my Uncle Chellappan's house at AIIMS quarters in Andrews Ganj, New Delhi. That's the time I came across a young cousin of mine- Bobby; though there was a huge age gap, he was my companion for the rest of the days that I stayed in Delhi. Our friendship made each other respect our thoughts, our ideas and became the link between our families.

Believe it or not, during those days he was a mischievous kid like any other normal kid. Being an elder son, he used to be punished more frequently by his dad than his younger brother, Robby, for the disorganized work or not fulfilling the task.

After 5 years I had been back to Delhi at Bobby's house as a part of my night stay as I was the technical crew of the Aircraft IL-76 from Indian Air Force station, Agra. Now, it became more frequent to visit their house whenever I used to land in Delhi. I do remember those days when Bobby used to take me to a few places such as Deer Park, Mehrauli etc. I could see the transition in him. He became very soft-spoken, smiling always and well-organized in his task and approach. He used to mingle with people, and ground to earth- a quality he must have acquired from his dad. Whenever I was in Delhi in their house, I used to also attend the fasting prayers along with him. It was a different kind of experience whenever I used to attend the prayers at their home, where I used to search for peace to overcome petty problems.

Once the whole Delhi group (his dad, mum, uncle, aunty, Bobby, Robby, Jobby etc.) had been to Bangalore to attend a mass Church gathering. We were blessed to have them all at our house. All the elders stayed at my mother's place and all the youngsters at my house.

Whenever Bobby visited Bangalore for his Church activities, he made his time to visit my mother's house to have the delicious meals prepared by my mother. I can't forget his smile at every sentence he spoke. I have never seen him lose his temper on any occasion, a character that only a blessed person will have.

Had an opportunity to be present with my family members for his marriage in Delhi. Bobby's marriage was a memorable and a lesson to be taken into our lives. The whole sequence of the marriage program was so well-planned, organized and coordinated. The introduction of bride and groom families, the prayers at appropriate places, the songs by the carol group, the dressing etc. a lesson to be carried along with us. It was the brain and tireless effort of Bobby who had organized the complete program of the marriage. He was blessed to have Blessy as his life partner who was very supportive of all his engagements in the

path of Church activities; always ready to sacrifice anything in her life to fulfill her husband's dreams and so were the family members of both the families. Also, he was blessed to have a son and daughter who made a complete circle of an ideal family filled with prayers and Church activities.

There is an old saying that "God takes away good people early than the aged people". It was true in the case of Bobby. The qualities exhibited by Bobby in others' lives are like the depth of the sea which cannot be measured easily.

With Love to my dear friend ....

Raju bhaiya

Cousin

FRIENDS

Friends

*D*ear Reader,

You are about to embark on a journey of a 21st Century Saint, Pastor Bobby Chellappan- a man who moved in the unction of the Holy Spirit. There will always be one Pastor Bobby, and only one Pastor Bobby. God's Servant Pastor Bobby was used mightily in our generation. I have known Pastor Bobby for several years since 1983 when his father and mother Pastor Chellappan and Sister Lalitha, Bobby, and Robby were residing in Ayurvigyan Nagar, Delhi. During the teenage years, we attended Vacation Bible School together and our families were closely knit together in the bond of love and spiritual fellowship.

We have had so many beautiful fasting and prayer sessions with the family all together. As I observe the formative years of Pastor Bobby during the early 90's, the man of God was anointed by the Power of the Holy Spirit. Life changed and a passion to serve Jesus Christ was birthed in his heart. Pastor Bobby couldn't wait for Sundays to be at the Church of God and even during weekdays, he used to preach the Gospel to everyone. And while he knew he was too young to lead the church, he also knew that somewhere there was something he could do for God.

As I fast forward to recent years, God used Pastor Bobby to pioneer Church Planting amongst the locals of New Delhi, pioneer in Television Media Ministry and Bible Translation Ministry along with teaching in Theological Seminaries. God's Church today needs men and women of God who have surrendered everything- their life, their might, and their all. God's ministry today needs ministers who are willing to spend and to be spent for His Kingdom.

In each generation, only a handful rise to special prominence as that of Pastor Bobby. This book is such an example of abandonment to God, characterized by total commitment, obedience, and selflessness. I pray that the pages of this book will challenge you to live a life of faith and do the impossible for God by the power of the Holy Spirit. May God enrich you as you read each chapter of this book with a prayerful heart and total abandonment to our Lord and Savior, Jesus Christ, who died for us and rose again on the third day.

Your brother in Christ,

Pastor David Simon OHIO,

USA

Bobby, my classmate in school, was a very dear friend to me. I remember him very fondly! Even though we got to know each other only in high school as we chose the same stream, he left a positive imprint on all his school friends. He was a very gentle soul, always very calm and composed. He also was very caring and empathetic and none of us ever had any complaints about him.

One thing I remember very vividly was his passion for basketball. He was an excellent sportsman with a great sportsman spirit. Whenever there was a free period, we could see him on the basketball court, sometimes even playing all alone. Even though he was slightly shorter than all the rest of the players, he was a good shooter.

After we left school, we couldn't stay well connected for a few years. I was later pleasantly surprised to know that he had left his job and stepped into ministry. I somehow did not perceive that Bobby would do that, but I was overjoyed by his decision. From then on, we were able to connect very often as we would get to meet each other during various meetings and events like prayer drives and many such gatherings in the city. I could see him as a person with a huge passion and a burden for souls.

He was also a very good Bible teacher. We were privileged to have him come and minister to the leadership team in our church a few times. He taught very systematically from the Bible and his messages were quite enlightening. Even during the lockdown, he gave an encouraging message online to our congregation from the life of Esther and that message is still imprinted on our hearts. We were privileged to have been able to support each other's ministries in various ways.He was a great encourager and motivator. He never failed to appreciate and encourage me each time I forwarded my newly recorded songs to him. His genuine encouragement and good wishes meant a lot.

Bobby was a multi-talented person and was able to accomplish a lot in different areas of ministry. He reached great heights in theological studies, did historic work in Bible translation, he was a renowned Bible school teacher, a prayer warrior, a good mentor, encourager, preacher, pastor and so many other things but at the same time a very humble and genuine servant of the Lord! This combination of greatness and humility is rare, but Bobby is an example of that.

I am grateful to God for his life and commitment and for the leadership he could give to the Body of Christ, not only in the city but to the larger body globally.

In a very short time, he became an influence in the Christian world.

Bobby and his memories along with his enchanting smile are something that I will carry to my grave. See you on the other shore my friend!

Persis John

All Nations House of Prayer (ANHOP)

I got a surprising message last week from our dear Sister Blessy Bobby which brought back many sweet memories we had with our dear Pastor Bobby Chellappan.

We first met Bobby's family in the 90s when we moved to Ayurvigyan Nagar in New Delhi as his mother, Sister Lalitha Chellappan and I worked in the Nephrology dept at AIIMS. At that time, Pastor Bobby was just a young teenager around 17 or 18 years of age. His parents were among the first to nurture us as new believers along with the Church we went to at that time - 'Delhi Revival Centre'. Very often, we would attend the prayer meetings at Pastor Chellappan's house which was instrumental in our growth as young Christians.

While at the meetings, we would notice Bobby spending time with his friend Jiju, sharing the good word and witnessing for Christ. Bobby was very involved in the youth leadership at their Pentecostal Church (Gilgal Bhavan) and the ICPF Organization. One of the things we learned from him was his decision to do the right thing, even when it was inconvenient. While driving around Delhi roads late into the night, he would always make it a point to stop at the red lights and wait for the green, something that was not usually followed by most drivers back then. It was something he taught us quite early on, the responsibility to always do the right thing, even when no one is around.

After moving out of AV Nagar, Pastor Chellappan and Pastor Bobby Chellappan obeyed God's command and started the Apostolic Faith Church with close family and other friends. It was such a blessing to attend their first Sunday fellowship meeting with other believers. Pastor Bobby eventually took over that Church and led it to new horizons, his ministry amongst the many lost souls in India would truly make his family and friends proud.

We eventually reconnected when Bobby came to Florida in 2013 and was gracious enough to minister to our Church here on youth meetings, cell group meetings and in Sunday Church meetings. We witnessed as the young teenage Bobby transformed into a powerful warrior of Christ on the pulpit, spreading the word across continents. During the pandemic period as all the Church meetings were held on Zoom, he was always ready to share and inspire our small group (Christ Family Fellowship) too. He didn't need any extra time to prepare the messages and even on short notice, was ready and always eager to share God's word. It was such a blessing for us to listen to Pastor Bobby for the inspiring words and testimony about the various challenges he faced during his lifetime. Truly a good and faithful servant of the Lord.

Bro. Santosh Franc

Florida, USA

With Santosh Franc Uncle and family and ministering in Florida, USA.

Pastor Bobby Chellappan was a man of God that I respect and honor so much. I met him over a decade ago at the Pentecostal fellowship meeting at Pastor Josh Kallimel's Church and ever since then, we got genuinely connected and became like bond brothers. Pastor Bobby was a very humble, sincere, devoted and committed servant of God who will never do anything for financial gain. He was such a man of God that always tried to see how he could be of help to you for you to fulfill your spiritual dreams and aspirations.

As a missionary and foreigner in India, I met so many pastors, but none could be compared to Pastor Bobby in terms of sincerity, humility, straightforwardness, and kingdom dedication. Pastor Bobby gave me and my ministry unusual support at every time required, even when it conflicted with his own ministry's timings and schedules. When it was apparent that I had to leave India, Pastor Bobby was the only trusted pastor who stood in the gap for me. For several months, he oversaw my ministry alongside his church, preaching at both ministries every Sunday, making sure that everything went well with the ministry in my absence without charging any rupees for his services. He never for once took advantage of my absence or leveraged his position as an Indian Pastor to convert or take over the church.

Pastor Bobby Chellappan was a relatable person, he never discriminated against either by the reason of the color of your skin, your caste, your wealth, or any background. As long as you are a child of God, he was ready to go with you to any length without looking back. His passion for God and evangelism blew my mind in the year 2012 when I informed him about the evangelistic Christian movie (RUPANTAR) that we were planning to shoot in Delhi to win souls for the kingdom of God. He was not only excited about it, but he also put in all his resources into it including his finances, time, and ministry; even his entire family got involved in the movie to the glory of God. Through his help, we were able to get the locations for the movie, cast and crew's welfare and security. All these were single-handedly handled by Pastor Bobby without any financial rewards attached to it. After the successful production of the movie in India, there was an urgent need for the final production to be done in Nigeria. I consulted with Pastor Bobby and immediately he agreed to travel with me to Nigeria. He left his wife, children and Church and followed me to Nigeria for the postproduction of the first HINDI CHRISTIAN EVANGELICAL MOVIE "*RUPANTAR*" produced by SHILOH GLOBAL WORSHIP CENTER IN CONJUNCTION WITH THE MOUNT ZION MOVIES INTERNATIONAL.

Pastor Bobby was a genuine believer that you could depend on his time as a brother, friend, and co-labourer in the vineyard of God. Each time he visited America, he would make sure that we met before his final departure to India. I know him to be a loving husband, a great teacher of the word, a relentless evangelist, a friend in deed and a passionate pastor. We miss him so much, but I know that he is in a better place now. It is my prayer that the wife and the children that he left behind harvest the fruits of his labor in Jesus' name.

PASTOR OLAOLU OLUFADE

THE GENERAL OVERSEER,

SHILOH GLOBAL WORSHIP CENTER WORLDWIDE.

Bobby Chellappan: A True Servant of Jesus Christ

My earliest memories of Bobby go back to the closing months of 1991 when I relocated to New Delhi from Lucknow after completing my MBA at Lucknow University & getting married to Nissy. Bobby was attending the Church of God in Hauz Khas with his parents & brother. Since Bobby was closer to my age as a young man, we developed a friendship that would last his lifetime. During those days Bobby was working for Cox & Kings in the travel industry. He was very interested in spiritual matters, and I remember having many long conversations with him about Christian living. During the time we were in New Delhi, Bobby & I maintained a very close relationship as we shared a mutual interest in spiritual matters, particularly in areas of evangelism & discipleship.

In June 1992, I had a terrible motorbike accident & was bedridden for over three months. During this period, I remember Bobby frequently visiting me in the hospital and home as he tried to keep me cheerful. He could empathize with my situation and his presence was a highlight for me while I was convalescing from my sickness. Soon afterward, I relocated to Doha, Qatar, to join Nissy, and for the next few years, we would keep in touch through telephone conversations.

In 1998, I relocated to the United States and kept in touch with Bobby off and on through the telephone. When I visited New Delhi in 2012, Bobby arranged for me to visit Grace Theological Seminary & meet with Dr. K.V. Paul Pillai, as well as speak in the chapel service of the Seminary. Bobby arranged for multiple worship meetings during which time I could share God's Word. I could sense that the hand of God was strong with Bobby, as he dedicated his life to the ministry even though he took care of his invalid father for many years. During that period, Bobby visited us in Atlanta and was a blessing to our Church as he spoke insightful thoughts from God's Word.

The last time Bobby preached to our Church was through a Zoom fasting prayer meeting in January 2021. His message was insightful & our Church was truly blessed by the Word that he shared with us. The last telephone conversation that I had with Bobby after that was remarkable. He mentioned to me about life being transitory & how much work was still left to be done.

I truly believe that in his short life, Bobby served God faithfully in his ministry. He was kind & good to everyone around him, particularly to his family, friends, and Church members. Our Lord Jesus would greet Bobby with the words: "Well done, good and faithful servant!" Bobby was faithful to his calling until the end & I wish to echo the words of Apostle Paul as he came to the end of his life, which is what Bobby would say about himself as well: "I have fought the good fight, I have finished the race, I have kept the faith. Henceforth there is laid up for me the crown of righteousness, which the Lord, the righteous judge, will award to me on that day, and not only to me but also to all who have loved his appearing." (2 Timothy 4: 7-8)

Peace & Blessings,

Shibu Cherian, D.Min., Ph.D.

Lead Pastor

Carolinas Christian Assembly

Charlotte, NC, USA

CHURCH ACQUAINTANCES

*I*t's a privilege to witness the anointing and influence of Dr Bobby Chellappan in our lives. It was not more than a month after we got married, I lost my job and the only source of income. I remember my commitment before marriage with my wife that "I and my family shall serve the Lord ". But suddenly, my focus turned to getting a job first, because I don't want my lady to think anything otherwise (because of loss of my job). Now 2 years had passed and we were in prayer and at the same time looking for a spiritual Church or a pastor who could help us in moving forward.

It happened that another pastor led us to the Apostolic Faith Church. Just one day before that, I read Deuteronomy 13 that says – 'Lord will not leave me nor forsake me.' The next morning in the Sunday service, the pastor preached out of the same scripture. That was a confirmation from the Holy Spirit that I had come to the right place.

Sunday after Sunday as we came close to pastor Bobby, I came to know that he had resigned from his well-paid job and dedicated himself to the Kingdom.

Then a thought came to me; I am looking for a job leaving my commitment secondary and here's a man who has left his job and moved himself into ministry.

This was the trigger point for me. That was the day I realized that he had something. And I decided that I will be obedient and faithful unto him rest of my life. No sooner I realized that he was mentoring me.

It was then 5 years since we were married and had no children. All diagnosis reports were normal. All who knew us were praying for us. Special prayers had been conducted for the miracle. Yet without results.

One fine day Pastor Bobby was mentoring me saying: how not to stagger when your prayers seem not been answered. Romans 4:20- by giving glory to God and knowing that God is able to do what He says.

I started to meditate on this scripture and amazingly within 1 year, Mamta, my wife, conceived. God's faithfulness was manifested through pastor Bobby one after another in my life.

As time passed, I still remember my commitment to the Lord and was praying that God would open a door for us to minister in His kingdom. One fine day as the Lord appointed, the pastor offered us to help in the Church in different positions and responsibilities. We were glad to be part of God's plan for this church. Again, it was an opportunity to work and grow under the mentorship of pastor Bobby.

By this time, I understand that our spiritual level has been shifting. There must be someone who should be lifting you in the kingdom. And for us pastor, Bobby was the one who lifted us up.

Under his mentorship, I have observed and learned that consistent prayer is a vital part of a leader. I have witnessed him praying the whole night on his knees, and have seen amazing results not only in the Church but also in personal life. Receiving revelations one after another. People's lives get changed just with a touch of prayer or sometimes only with a word. It was something like Jesus was moving with him physically. Even though there was turmoil in the church, he led a prayerful life and overtook everything easily.

He was a door opener to many. A person who trained (practically) many to step into ministry. I had a desire to serve the Lord but didn't know where to start with. One fine Sunday service he asked me to help him in the Church administration.

That was the first opportunity for me to serve in the kingdom. On the other side, I also got an opportunity to come close to him. Learning things like, how to pray for Church finances, leaders, givers and for non-givers. Being in this position, God revealed many things about the hearts of people and to counsel them with the Word.

Again, after a few years he opened another door for me. It was our anniversary, and he came to my house, anointed my head with oil and declared my spiritual shifting to a prophetic office. That was the day I entered the next dimension of ministry. I stepped into the prophetic realm. The desire to have the gift of prophecy started to burn in my heart. Needless to say, he was the one who trained me and guided me to the realm of prophetic, to live a life of prophesy.

He anointed my head with oil and my cup runneth over. Now I realize that without having anything in my life, because of this oil that runneth over, I am an influence in the Church, in the family and everywhere.

Dr Bobby Chellappan is not just a name, but he is a treasure of blessings.

Lesson after lesson and glory after glory I have seen and learned through his life. In other words, I have seen the Holy Spirit moving through him in bodily form.

Sudhir Lima

Servant in His Kingdom

Apostolic Faith Church

Bobby bhaiya

To describe Bobby bhaiya for me is like a user manual for human beings given by God. The Bible is our user manual given to us by God but it is written in words. On the other hand, bhaiya was the practical movable version of God made User Manual that we could see, learn, and touch. He was the perfect example of Christ in today's date. Whatever I feel, think, and believe about Christ is because of Bobby bhaiya.

His spectacular teaching of Christ didn't allow me to look anywhere beyond Christ. He not only shared Jesus with me but implanted his teachings and faith in me deep in my heart. Bhaiya's character is what inspires me to live my life to the same standards. Love is not a feeling, but a choice, was taught well by Bobby bhaiya. To me, Bobby bhaiya was a true replica of Jesus. I love u bhaiya. Will meet soon over the shores.

My First Meeting with bhaiya

I still remember meeting bhaiya for the first time in October 2009. I was battling suicidal thoughts, and my friend Tapan took me to his house in the evening, to make me hear the gospel. And when Bobby bhaiya started to share the gospel with me, I was experiencing freedom in my heart. In one hour of meeting with him, I decided to follow Jesus all my life. I was wearing some astrological rings and at that moment I took it out and threw it in the dustbin. What power and anointing he used to carry and the way he used to speak was purely divine.

My Parents' first encounter with God.

It was Christmas and my parents had come from Kolkata to see me and I took them to attend my Church Christmas Function. My parents knew the Gospel, but they were not convinced of Jesus as the only way. But that day when Bobby bhaiya started to preach and share the Gospel and started to speak with his anointing, I saw that my parents were in tears and immediately after the meeting they accepted Christ. This was the Holy Spirit manifesting powerfully behind Bobby bhaiya.

Preaching Gospel by His Character.

We are often told to preach the gospel, but he used to live the Gospel. He was a true representation of Jesus Christ. He always had a smile on his face. I never saw him upset. Every challenge and situation he used to face with a big smile and faith. He was not only a true disciple, but a true leader for us too. The foundation that he laid on my heart for Christ is unshakable. He always used to take a stand for me and always used to encourage me to think Big … He knew the Bible so well…

He was perfect in all relationships- as a pastor, a great obedient son, a loving husband, a caring father, a strong pastor and a spiritual father for so many of us… I don't find anyone like you. How come you were so perfect?? You were indeed brilliant…

Dear God,

I thank you for introducing me to Bobby bhaiya. I don't know without him I would have known you so well. But because of him God, I know you and I love you. And I know, you have called him early because you wanted to give him some top positions in heaven to manage. He was a good manager, too. Lord, we thank you for eternity because we all can meet him one day on the other shore. Thank you, Jesus!

Subhojeet

Apostolic Faith Church

I still remember meeting Bobby bhaiya in a prayer meeting in RK Puram Sector 1, New Delhi at Shashi Uncle's house. I guess it was the year 1997-98 and I was in the 7th standard. I started going to the Church which was in the same building where he lived in Hauz Rani, New Delhi.

I started growing in Christ through him as the word says, "Without me you can't meet my father." That's exactly the way I met our living God Lord Jesus Christ through Bhaiya. He started putting his trust in me by giving me some small responsibilities in the church. Sometimes I succeeded in matching his expectations and a lot of times I failed. Through him, I learned how to grow in Christ as I grew up watching, working, and growing in Christ.

He has done so many things for me and my family that can't be described; he was there when my father left me and my family, he was there with me when I wasn't able to get admission in my senior secondary school, he was there to help me to find my life partner. There are thousands and millions of things he has done for me and my family and for all of us. As a person, he was the most stylish person and yet the simplest person I have come across till day. He never judged anyone, he had a very calm personality and I have never seen him getting angry or losing His patience in more than 2 decades of life spent with Bhaiya.

I never got the opportunity to tell him what he meant to me as I never had the courage to do so when he was there with us. But today, when I know he is not with us, I would like to tell him that he was my Godfather when my father was not beside me. When I needed him the most, Bhaiya was there for me. He was my mentor when no one was there to guide me. He was my big brother to scold me whenever I was wrong. He was a good friend also to me, whenever I needed any advice or wanted to share any problems. And as he was my pastor too, he upheld me and my family in prayers. Whenever we needed him, he stood up for us as he did for many people and families.

Again, I want to give thanks to the Lord for his life and his teachings which will help all of us to stand firm in front of His throne at the end.

I would like to share a few lines about my experience and journey with me about him as follows: -

Noor-E-Jahan (Light of the world)

A poem dedicated to bhaiya

He was my Noor-e-Jahan (light of the world)
Who illuminated all of us.
As soon as he was extinguished,
Darkness prevailed in the earth.

Had a good heart, clear faith, sweet tongue, pure soul,
Such a person, whoever knew him, became his own.
While walking on the God's way,
Countless people learned to follow his tone.

By marking his presence in everybody's need
Provided by God, he met their need.
Seeing such generous life, he lived
God Himself might have been happy indeed.

In childhood, when I lost my father,

He caught hold of my hand,

Showed me the right way,

Guided me how to live and stand.

In my each and every critical situation,

He was my guide.

By the word of God, he taught me

How to live as a good fighter.

When I felt the absence of my father

He acted as a shadow of him.

All my sorrows, afflictions, short-comings, mistakes

Concealed under his loving stream.

Whatever I am today,

I am because of him.

He taught me to live in such a way,

Enabled me to know the various mysteries of God's regime.

Look what happened,

When he left me alive.

We were taught to live better,

I thank God for his life.

I was taught to discriminate,

Every good and bad thing.

Because of his love and prayer

I was able to get rid of all conditioning.

By his smiling lips

He always took away river of sorrows.

A storm of trouble that was always stopped,

By dint of his powerful ethos.

He taught us to tide against the stream of sorrows,

Keeping strong faith in God.

He taught us how to have unwavering faith in God,

While Satan tries to trap us in its chord.

He was faithful to God to his last breath

And that is why he received the crown of life.

Who and how the reliable people are to be,

He showed the mirror by his face alive.

He was freely telling us secret of valuable words,

Out of which few were complete, few silent

Caused a great loss upon us,

By which our spiritual damage was very prominent.

Patience, love, and forgiveness

He showed us by living his life.

An inspiration to all of us

When we are bound to survive.

His deep conversation and long encounters

Or those cold nights of December of every 31st December

A golden era of pleasant phase

Went away along with his sudden departure.

He was a good servant of man,

In the form of human art

Whose journey was long.

Whose flight was high like a bird.

He had great knowledge of word of God,

He always stood strong by uttering amen.

Never failed even for a moment

His journey was difficult from earth to heaven.

He told us

How to set our destination

His life was so precious to follow,

Even God also needed him with His intervention.

Though God called him to Himself

According to His need

While going away from us,

He introduced us with God's eternity indeed,

Light of the world was mine

Its illumination was so tall.

As soon as it was extinguished.

Darkness prevailed in us all.

After you, it'll never be the same life again bhaiya as it was with you; will miss you bhaiya forever and ever. I'm sorry that I did not have the courage to say this to you when you were there but today let me say it to you that I love You bhaiya n you'll be there in my heart forever n ever. Love you and miss you a lot …. Always.!!!

Shibu
Apostolic Faith Church

I come from a Hindu background, and I visited different temples to get answers and solutions for my own life and family issues. Yet I did not get any solutions and was depressed and worried. Looking at all these one of my neighbors who is a Christian told me to try once at church. Obeying her I went along with her to Apostolic Faith Church (Delhi), where Pastor Bobby was preaching. My first experience in the Church was amazing and I felt peace inside my heart and realized that I have come to right place. My journey in Christ began with Pastor Bobby and his wife Pastor Blessy. I call them bhaiya and didi, they laid the foundation of Christ in me and have a great contribution to my spiritual life and my personal life as well.

From day one when I first went to Apostolic Faith Church, in fact, this was the first Church I ever went to; I had so much burden in my life be it my career, my family problems and the bondages of darkness. I shared a little bit of it with Bobby bhaiya and he smiled and said- "Don't worry, let's pray". Then he laid his hands on my head and started praying. Blessy di was also praying along with him with tears in her eyes for me and I was touched by the Holy Spirit and all the heaviness and fear within me was removed that day. I continued to go to Church and as I was a new believer didi used to teach me how to read the Bible, worship, how to pray etc. bhaiya used to encourage me to pray more, read bible more and listen to sermons to know the Word deeply. Soon I came to know about the baptism of the Holy Spirit and water baptism, and I wanted to receive it.

Then one fine day in Church bhaiya gave an altar call to receive the baptism of Holy Spirit. I also went in front along with others and he laid hands on me, and I received the Holy Spirit that day and started speaking in tongues. After a few months, I took water baptism also given by him. God also used him as a prophet in my life, one of the prophecies he made over me was "This is just a platform for you, don't stick to it God has a greater plan for you". At that time, I didn't understand but later I saw this prophecy fulfilled in my life. As a person, bhaiya was so humble and compassionate, full of the Holy Spirit, an anointed man of God.

On the personal side bhaiya was like a father figure to me. Looking at my situations, bhaiya and didi were always concerned about my personal life, and careful that everything was going well with me. I still remember when the proposal for my marriage came, I was worried about how it would be done. Since I came from a Hindu background my parents were not bold enough to come forward for the marriage because of the society pressure. That time bhaiya and didi took me to their home to stay. Not only that, didi took so much care of me in matters related to food, buying things for wedding, parlour etc. She made scrub for me and used to apply it over me herself, so that I may look good and healthy as I prepared for my wedding day.

At that time, I was going through financial difficulty since I was not getting support from my own family because of religious issues. At that time bhaiya and didi came forward and spent a lot of money without even letting me know about my wedding. They did not let me realize if I had any problems or difficulties, they took care of every small and big thing which I needed most at that time. And this is to them from my heart- "You were always there for me in my ups and downs. Thank you so much bhaiya and didi for all that you both have done for me. Many words of 'thanks' are not enough to express my gratitude. You built the foundation of Christ in my life. You both showed me a new life in Christ. Your instructions and guidance have always been a help to me. Not only me but you have impacted the lives of thousands. Unable to accept your sudden demise – bhaiya! It has made a great void in us.... You will always be in our hearts. I miss you, bhaiya!"

As a mentor and spiritual guide, bhaiya taught me how to live a life of testimony which he had set an example for others. Not only to live for yourself, but for others also whether it be praying with elders of the Church or giving counsel to youngers or helping those who are in a difficult situation all these helped me to serve in the new Church where I am now since my marriage.

In the new Church my Sr. Pastor appointed me as youth leader and I came across many young girls who were having difficulties spiritually, family issues and other challenges which I too had before. As I had learned from bhaiya I could give counsel to such young girls and encouraged them to abide in Christ in all situations and they were comforted. Apart from this in other areas also I could serve the Church. For all these, I sincerely thank Bobby bhaiya for his contribution to my life which made me from nothing to something.

Anubha Jyotish
Victory Church, New Delhi

A thank you note for my beloved pastor.

Even though there are so many people who become a part of your life, finding such a genuine, loving and caring person like you, pastor, is very rare.

You have always fed your flock so well with the word of God and out of them I'm one who was so hungry for his kingdom. By your preaching you drew me closer and closer to Christ as a result I could enjoy a deeper relationship with Jesus and taste his love even more.

I always miss the word FOCUS that you used to quote in your message while preaching and I could explicitly see your focus and dependency on God and God alone for everything. By becoming a spiritual father to every one whosoever came to you in search of love you won their heart.

You have worked so hard daily to convey the message of God for His sheep. Thank you for the people you have brought to Christ and for the disciples you nurtured.

Pastor, you were the true reflection of God; who's heart was always after God's will regardless of the challenges you had faced for his name's sake. You finished your race so well and became an inspiration for us to do the same.

Thank you for helping the Church grow in the love of God pastor and showing the true love of Christ to us.

Miss you pastor. I wish I could tell you these words meeting you in real. You are my spiritual father and will always be.

Yours Church member,

Geetu

There was a great move of the Holy Spirit in the 1990s, when we were praying the whole night and fasting prayers for the revival of the nation. God told us about the coming revival which will change the nation's spirituality, economically and socially.

In those days there were many people staying at our home during the fasting prayers. The schedule was like this- morning prayer at 5 am. Then the main session started at 9 am, which went on until 1 pm. Then again 2 pm intercessory prayer. The evening session started at 6 pm and went on until 9 pm. Then when everyone wanted to sleep, Pastor Bobby and Thomachayan, Bangalore would come straight from the office to start the next session. When these fiery men reached, we never wanted to sleep. We always remember those wonderful days, full of passion and life for Christ.

Bobby was well honored in the place of his work. He has worked in the secular and in the Christian field as a faithful and skilled professional. During the beginning years of his ministry, while he was still too young, he had to manage responsibilities in the office and in the ministry. He was more mature than most of his age. A man full of wisdom. We always looked to him for Godly wisdom and advice during our initial years of ministry. Even if he was younger in age, we looked to him as our elder brother.

He had a thorough knowledge of the Word of God. He knew how to balance between the word knowledge/ teaching of the word and the manifestation/ gifts of the Holy Spirit. Bobby was an apostle, a prophet, and a good Bible teacher. I think he finished his work early and went home.

I got the opportunity to travel with him for many meetings and conferences around the world. We always had something to learn from him. We will never forget the contribution he made to our personal Christian life and ministry.

Bobby had gone through many pains when his father, Pastor Chellappan went through many years of treatment and lost his leg and later passed away. Later his mother also passed away after being in bed for a long time. But during all these times he showed the endurance of a mature disciple. He was never tired of all the hardships he had to go through and all the responsibility that was on his shoulders. He had a divine strength that kept him focused on what God put into his trust.

We will see all the prayers of Bobby answered. Bobby will see it from heaven and rejoice over it. If you love him, continue to pray, and live for saving the lost souls of this nation and Bobby will rejoice with us in heaven. One day as we all reach there on that beautiful shore; we will be able to rejoice with him in the presence of God.

Pastor K.R. Abraham

Masih Ghar,
Devli, New Delhi

With Pastor K.R. Abraham and family, Pastor Chandy Varghese and family and Bro. Gaurav and family after a fellowship dinner.

This is in honor of Dr. Bobby Chellappan, a great friend of mine. God has made it possible for us to establish a bond that cannot be broken.

If my memory serves me well, Pr. Bobby traveled to Bhopal, M.P., with his team (Pr. Chandy, Pr. Abraham, etc.), to pray for this region. God powerfully talked to us via his workers and about the condition of Bhopal. The team then visited our home, where we spent some time in prayer. After that, I learned that Pr. Bobby is a man of prayer, and as a result, our friendship grew much stronger. We had a strong spiritual love in this regard. I experienced a strong sense of love and affection for Pr. Bobby among everyone in the room. I always felt that he was completely enveloped in God's love whenever he spent time with me or spoke to me. He didn't ever spend time telling jokes. He applied himself with great sincerity and diligence to the task that God had given him.

He frequently traveled to Bhopal and assisted us in a variety of ways, particularly in our missions and ministries. Even God has enabled me to reside at his home, pray, and participate in the ministry that God has given him. His parents, wife (Blessy), and kids lived with him in heaven, which served as their home.

He was quite involved in Zoom even throughout the COVID era, and he frequently joined us virtually in Church gatherings. His remarks usually contained profound substance and were encouraging. He had a heavy burden for the people of India, and he constantly prayed and begged God for assistance. For the glory of God, may the load Pr. Bobby carried be passed to his wife and children.

Dear Good friend, I sincerely hope that we will soon cross paths in heaven.

Rev. Biju Varghese

A.G Presbyter

Bhopal (M.P)

I met Pastor Bobby in 2017 when we relocated to Delhi NCR. The first introduction I had of this amazing man of God was a very simple exchange of greeting and the brief that he was a senior pastor and faculty associated with Life Christian University in India.

A year later we were very privileged to have Pastor Bobby visit our Delhi campus as faculty to teach various subjects. In our short association in the next 2 and a half years, Pastor Bobby's life, ministry, and character became evident to me in different instances, from the witness of those whose lives he had left an indelible mark.

His service and exploits are great in number and impact, beyond what could be put into a lifetime of any ordinary man his age. I remember being very amazed to know his age during his home going ceremony. Pastor Bobby was an unassuming man with much dignity, wisdom, and maturity. His calm yet confident demeanor, with a soft-spoken voice and a sweet smile, did not lack the caliber of high-level leadership and a simple life of faith and wisdom to juggle his numerous commitments with utter poise and meticulous planning. He packed so many years of life on earth and finished his race with so much more speed than most could ordinarily accomplish.

Integrity and Fearlessness were his hallmarks, and that was evident in his walk. I remember a couple of conversations we had over the years mostly regarding his availability for teaching schedules. I got to know only then about his vast responsibilities, and the humility with which he performed his duties. I will always treasure his words of encouragement, kindness, and wisdom that have inspired me. There are countless lives he has touched, destinies that he has guided, and relationships that he nurtured and ministered to along with his precious wife and beautiful soulmate Blessy.

In these lives, his legacy of love for God and service to His people will live on. We remember you fondly Pastor Bobby, and are confident with joyous hope in our hearts, that we will see you on the other side of the shore. We are grateful to God for your life that was lived in honor of your Savior and God.

Sis. Christine Som

Life Christian University(LCU) Co-ordinator

Saket Campus, New Delhi

Dr. Bobby Chellappan

The sudden home calling of Pastor Bobby was a rude jolt to many of us. We never had any clue that a life with so much of talents and potentialities would be plucked away from the earth just like that. Yet it has pleased the Master of the Universe to do so. The born-again life belongs to the Master, and He alone has the sole right to call for it whenever He needs it in His Magnificent Presence. All Glory to Him and to Him alone who sits on the throne. Pastor Blessy asked me whether I would be able to write a few words about Pastor Bobby for the book that she has been planning to release. I agreed to do it at once even without any second thought. The reason being that he had been a good friend to me in the body of Christ.

There are many things that I could think of Pastor Bobby. But a few things stand tall when I remember about him.

He was a man of passion. Anything that was given to him, he took it, owned it, worked on it and brought it to fruition. And that too without any show of a sense of pride but with humility and simplicity. Yes, simplicity was a part of him. He was not a man of complexities. Passion was the foundation of his life on earth.

He never abandoned his passionate love for God and the things of God. Whether this was translations or traveling to present the Good News to the suffering masses or taking training sessions for the potential and emerging leaders, he was at the best of his Godly passion. Leadership Training and equipping the Leaders had been his paramount priority of ministry. Pastor Bobby had well understood that if the field is to be harvested, the job needs harvesters. That was why he spent more time equipping and transforming the potential leaders.

He was also a visionary. His vision joined with the right Leadership Groups, has made it possible for thousands of people to be blessed in many ways. He did something in the TV programs, presenting the Good News to the digital world. His enthusiasm for making the Hindi Bible available in audio form was something to be praised. After having done so many things, he has never bragged about his achievements.

As far as I am concerned, I have never come across any time where I could feel that he was bragging about anything, big or small. He had been always humble and gave glory to God. He was a man of easy access. Accessibility was one of his characteristics. Every time he joined us either in the Delhi Transformation Network

(DTN) Monthly meetings or in the GDOP (Global Day of Prayer) events, he took a special interest in praying and sharing the word and his experiences for the edification of the City Leaders.

Humanly speaking, it is sad that he left us all. But as mature believers, we just leave it to the will of God. It is our humble prayer that the ministry that he started for the extension of the Kingdom of God, would continue to grow and would be able to raise many Leaders who would take the vision to the heights. May God bless Pastor Blessy and the family and the Church members as they keep the legacy of Dr. Bobby Chellappan.

With many prayers,

Dr YD Jeyaseelan,
President,

Victory Churches of India,
D-120, Dr Ambedkar Colony,
Andheria Mode, Chattarpur PO,
New Delhi-110074.

Occasionally, you come across a man who leaves a lasting impression on you. My friend Bobby was such a man who truly followed the Lord with all his heart. When I think about him it causes gratitude to arise in my heart that God gave me a friend like him. He was the man of his word.

When we read in the scriptures, we find that Laban was blessed because of Jacob, and Egypt was blessed because of Joseph. So many times, even after King David's death, God spared His people for the sake of His King David.

Because of the faith of four friends, Jesus healed the paralytic who was brought to Him by his friends. Bobby was surely one such man because of whom God changed many lives.

I had the privilege of knowing him personally; we had been part of many mission trips together. When I preached, he translated; when he preached, I translated; there was never a dull moment around him. He was always hungry for the Lord. His faith was rock solid. He served willingly to young and old alike. To a friend, he was a friend who would stick closer more than a brother would. One of the best things I liked about him was that he was never jealous of another man's success. In fact, he would labor intensely so that others would become successful. I have seen many whom he disciples stand on his shoulders and look tall, but he was never weary of bearing their weight. Some thanked him and acknowledged his investment in their lives, but many used him and left, some even abused him; but irrespective of what others did to him, he remained loyal to his God, his family, his ministry, and his calling.

He dedicated the last decade of his life to translation of the Bible and the advancement of that work. He was committed to serve. He created a legacy that will continue till the Lord Jesus returns. Many languages which never had the Bible translated are having it now because of what Bobby did. To a theologian, he was a theologian; to a common man he was a common man. He truly embodied what Apostle Paul confessed I have become all to all so I might win some to Christ.

Once I was invited to a place called Bijapur in Chattisgarh, a notorious place known for all sorts of crime. The place was dominated by Naxals. It was a dangerous place where life was at risk for preaching the gospel. I was invited to conduct a gospel crusade there. I felt the Lord said yes to me to go. However, I was too scared to go. So, I approached my friends if they would join me for the Gospel crusades for five days. It was amazing that all my friends said yes to me and traveled at their expense just to be with me. They were not preaching nor were they ministering, but they just came to be with me. It was incredible for what they had done for the sake of friendship. Pas. Bobby Chellappan, Pas. Abraham KR, Pas. Chandy Varghese, Pas. Moses David, Pas. Girish Daga were such encouragement to me. They stood their ground with me until we saw the place transformed with the love of Christ. There was such an incredible unity among brothers that nothing seemed impossible. Everyone was eager to serve each other. From preaching to 10000s to cleaning toilets, nothing was beyond our ability to do sincerely. There I observed Bobby for 5 days- a man indeed of few words but a golden heart. He served like Jesus wasn't ashamed to wash dishes, broom the room, polish others' shoes, clean up toilets, teach at Pastors conferences and did all without any complaints. The joy of the Lord overflowed his heart like a fountain.

Whether an American or an illiterate villager, Bobby remained the same and served both with integrity of heart and skillfulness of hands. I remember when we would pray, the way God would give us prophetic directions through him was incredible. The whole team benefited hugely because of him. With him standing with me I felt stronger. I miss him.

Sometimes, when I would be going through challenging times, I would call him and irrespective of his busyness he would take time out just for me. He would hear me out, counsel me, and pray with me. We would joke & laugh together, then would ride together to pick up Pas. Abraham and Chandy and just be together. There was this sense of belongingness that crossed all the barriers of differences we had had in our upbringing.

Even though he was battling a challenging time at his own home where he had to take care of his father who was chronically ill and was dependent on him, Bobby never shunned his domestic responsibilities. He would be concerned and still be compassionate for those who sought his help. I still wonder how he could manage it all so well.

I was honored to know him as a dear friend and a teacher who taught me for my B.Th. studies. His memories inspire me to go deeper with the Lord and serve with integrity of heart. I have read that true success in ministry is when the ministry continues to grow in your absence under the leadership of those whom you raised during your tenure of service, and now my eyes see it happening in my friend Pas. Bobby's ministry. Every work he pioneered continues to grow and bear much fruit even in his absence.

He caught the vision early, He fought a good fight of faith, and he loved till the last.

Truly a life well spent for the cause of the gospel of Lord Jesus Christ.

I am grateful for his wife Pas. Blessy and both his children who gave me this honor to pen down my thoughts about him. May His biological and spiritual children continue to see the fulfillment of all that God promised him in Jesus's name. Amen!

Ps. Joshua David
Father's Touch ministries

COLLEAGUES

It has been a real blessing for me to get to know Dr. Bobby Chellappan ever since he joined BCS. I always enjoyed our time together although he was a man with few words, humble and soft-spoken.

I remember several occasions when we met together in the BCS office as well as in the Ashram and our long hours of fellowship, discussions, and planning.

We had the joy of working together in the CCBT movement, especially about to the gateway language translations. Dr. Bobby worked closely with our translation team in Punjabi and Urdu languages which resulted in the timely completion of the project with high quality.

We are sorry that his ministry has been abruptly cut down. However, we have a great assurance that we will meet him again in our Father's presence. He has fought a good fight, he kept his faith, finished his race and he has already received the crown of righteousness.

Dr. Alex Abraham
Operation Agape

Dr. Bobby Chellappan - a life beautifully lived for God and his word:

Dr. Bobby was an extraordinary man of God who served faithfully and effectively during his life in a variety of roles and contexts before he went to be with the Lord in 2021. Friends, family, and Church family all over the world are still shocked and in deep sorrow about his going to be with Jesus, way before any of us imagined.

He wore many hats and excelled in those; I am writing this about my experiences with him in the ministry of the Bible Translation which I had the privilege of working alongside for over half a decade. Bobby joined this ministry in late 2015 and spearheaded the first large-scale implementation of a global strategic vision for translation into languages of wider communication (called Gateway languages) in the subcontinent. The Indian Revised Version in over a dozen major languages, now published on www.vachanonline.com is the result of his team's efforts. Additionally, he set up large translation teams that work in several domains' scripture, commentaries, exegetical material, stories, audio and video, and software localization – for dozens of languages in this country and beyond.

Towards the end of his life and untimely death, one of the significant contributions he made was the Indian Sign Language (ISL) translation work, the work involved the creation of a sign language token dictionary, translation of the first full Bible into ISL in six years, which many thought was too ambitious, but he had the courage to say it's possible with God; and the project is going on well today in with extensive involvement and ownership of the deaf communities, churches from many states of India whom he connected with and invited to be part of what God is doing.

His gifting and ability to connect Church networks and ministry leaders in the country and globally was quite evident – he would travel to visit seminaries, denomination heads, and organizational leaders regularly to every corner of the country and internationally too. Bobby was a people person as most of us know, and his ability to connect and develop great friendships that later could become ministry partnerships was very evident. Bobby was a true game-changer; through his effective networking with local and global Church networks, the ministry of translation of God's word into the remaining Bible-less peoples of this part of the world can be achieved in the not-too-distant future.

While the world relies a lot on technology, tools, and pure innovation – Bobby still depended on prayer. His prayer life and witness were an example to many of us who got the privilege to serve alongside him. As a person, he was seldom seen as anxious or rushed in any way even handling very large amounts of people, projects, and deadlines. His quiet but confident nature stood out, as he seemed to not trust in mere words or human wisdom but in the grace of God to help accomplish great things for the Lord. If he was asked a difficult question about a project or work, he would just smile and say – let's see what God does!

He knew what his calling was, he quietly worked on it and accomplished things that people had rarely attempted – all without making a big deal about it. While we still grieve and don't understand the why of Dr. Bobby's passing, we do celebrate a life lived well and a rich and inspiring legacy for God and the Church and people he cared about.

Dr. Binu Alexander

I met Pastor Bobby first time when I was in sixth class, at a Christmas program at a school in Chandanhola, New Delhi. He was anchoring the event. I was one of the participants in that event. I was very amazed by the way he dressed up and anchored the whole program. That first meeting is still fresh in my mind, and I still carry the picture of the pastor of that event.

After a few years of that event, I got an opportunity to join his church. I was in the youth group where I was involved in the worship team. A day before Sunday worship, our group used to stay late at night for practice. And Pastor Bobby and his wife Blessy Didi, always visited us late at night in the church, guiding and teaching us how to grow in our spiritual life. That was the time when I came closer to him and started knowing about him more. Due to his continuous guidance, my spiritual life was getting stronger.

I remember one incident; Pastor Bobby and I were coming back home from a prayer meeting. And a famous Hindi gospel song "Rajadhi Raja Mahima Ke Sath" came across my mind. I happened to ask him if he knew the song. And he said yes and sang the whole song with great joy for me while driving. I was deeply impacted by this incident as being a famous pastor and influential leader he humbled himself and did not hesitate to sing to glorify the Lord.

Another opportunity was when I got to work with him by joining the same office where he was the General Manager. I worked directly under his leadership. At work, whenever I faced any challenges, I could freely approach him, and I knew that he would provide me with solutions. He always motivated, directed, and counseled me to perform better and work on developing my skill sets. His way of dressing, speaking, and behaving with people has influenced me and helped me to do better in life.

It is a blessing that Pastor Bobby also solemnized my marriage. I am honored and grateful to him. I am among the most blessed ones who had an opportunity to spend the maximum time with Pastor Bobby and learn about his life closely.

He was not only my pastor, mentor, and big brother but my boss as well. He has invested in my life through his knowledge, teachings, and time. There is no single day when I do not remember him and his teachings. He has been a strong pillar of support in my life.

He was the humblest, pure-hearted and immensely patient person, I have ever met. I thank God for bringing him into my life and I am greatly blessed.

Love you, dearest bhaiya!

Sunil Robert

Pastor Bobby Chellappan- a man of God walking in impeccable faith, having immense patience even in storms, an influential orator, a motivator with excellent leadership skills, a great listener, and a very good human being with a kind heart.

For many, he was a pastor, bhaiya, and teacher but for me, he was the **"best boss"** ever.

As he had impacted several lives, so was my life deeply impacted. I met him for the first time at BCS Office. I am among those privileged ones who got the chance to work with Pastor Bobby under his guidance.

Working with him closely helped me to learn, how to handle stressful work situations calmly, take up new responsibilities and perform with excellence. I used to sit in the same room where he sat. And I observed that as he was the General Manager and took care of the translation department, every member used to report to him and shared their challenges and difficulties with him. He always counseled, comforted, and guided them to stay motivated in life. No matter how big we felt our problems were, he was there to provide the solution.

Under his leadership, every one of us felt very protected and secure. We were confident that if we made mistakes, he would wait for us to learn from them. He would never be impatient and hard on us.

I am very blessed that I got a lifetime opportunity to work with him, though for a very short span.

I was amazed that Pastor Bobby was an awesome actor as well. I watched his film Rupantar, a faith movie and was mesmerized by his acting skills.

His sermons used to be very detailed and always eye-opening and life-changing. Even a non-believer would show interest in hearing and would start thinking about what he spoke and would want to know more about Jesus.

One day at the office during lunch, he mentioned that he was also a faculty at one of the Bible colleges and taught subjects related to hell. He said that "hell is real". I asked him how it felt in hell. He told me that light a gas burner at your home and put your finger on that and you would know how it feels. It was funny yet a good way to learn.

In the same office, I met my husband, Sunil. And I was very impressed by the fact that he was from Pastor Bobby's Church and is very close to him. I thought that Sunil has seen his life closely and he might also reflect his character. This fact made my decision to marry Sunil. The greatest blessing was that Pastor Bobby solemnized our marriage which my husband and I will always cherish.

I always remember him when I get impatient or angry about something at work or in life and think if Sir had been here now, how would he have dealt with the situation? And then there is a sudden change in the attitude I find in myself. He lived life to show Christ-like character and stand firm in the faith. He has set an example to love God and live a faithful life.

He is an unforgettable treasure who changed many lives, saved souls, and worked hard for God's kingdom. His calm and sweet smiling face always remains in my eyes and many unforgettable memories in my heart.

Always miss you Sir!

Jyoti Sunil

Dr. Bobby Chellappan

First I met Dr. Bobby Chellappan at Keystone, South Dakota, USA during September 2013. We both were attending the Disciple-making training program with other trainees. He was a sincere first bench student and sat in the first line throughout the training. He was friendly to all and was very humble with always a cute smile.

After the training, we went on our respective paths, but Dr. Bobby kept on communicating through encouraging spiritual messages mostly via email.

After a few years in 2016 in March, we met in Delhi as I was selected for the Gujarati Bible Translation Project. When he came to know that the organization that he was working in was considering my name to lead the Gujarati Bible Translation Project, he strongly recommended my name to lead the project.

As the Project began, Dr. Bobby came to Gujarat and stayed at my house. His presence was encouraging to me, the project staff and to my family too. He shared his testimony and messages from the Word of God with us. He motivated us to do the Bible translation effectively. He took out time to encourage my family too. I am remembering a sentence he told me i.e. "Before God accomplishes His plan for you, He will not call you into His eternal rest." I am sure that God completed His purpose through the life of Dr. Bobby, before calling him into His eternal rest.

I miss him. He was a good friend, a good preacher, a very good counselor and a nice leader.

Wilson Jacob
Gujarat

Do you see a man skilled in his work? He will stand before kings; He will not stand before obscure men. Prov 22: 29.

Dr Bobby's home call is one of the most puzzling of such calls in recent times. Why should he receive such an untimely call (unless the Lord needed him to assist in administration in heaven!!). We all have lost a true friend, an efficient handler of people and a true man of God.

First and foremost, I know him as the greatest handler of people. It is, by no means, an easy task to deal with more than a dozen of the best of Christian literature professionals of the land; and that, too, for three whole years!

More than that, he made each language manager feel that he was the only partner of GLS pan India. Of course, I know that he was running with a dozen more groups like ours. I found it amazing, the attention, focus and value he gave to me (and I know that he gave the same feeling to the managers of projects of all GLS languages).

Due to a few sporadic glimpses into his ministry, I got to know that he was a multi-talented, multi-tasking person of multiple intelligences. Be it pastoring, movie production, preaching and managing an international office in Delhi city, and projects pan India.

A man becomes a man only by his intelligence, but he was a man only by his heart. Dr Bobby was a fine and fabulous balance of brain and heart.

He was a good man. A good man shares his knowledge selflessly with everyone. He was patient and warm, answering all kinds of questions and offering solutions to all the issues that kept cropping up. Never had I to wait for more than a day, to receive an answer to my emails. And he never allowed to lapse more than an hour to call back in case he could not pick up my call. And he always provided me with appropriate and purposeful answers and suggestions with great generosity and kindness of heart.

Dr Bobby always made me feel special, always conveying the feeling that he (and the organization that he was working with) was grateful for my participation in the translation project, while I was the one who was immensely grateful to them for the rare opportunity of managing the Telugu GLS project. I am not sure how much planning and contemplation went into the project, but when it was presented to us, it was flawless. Execution, handholding, and finances were impeccable. I see Dr Bobby's hand in the entire structure of the project. I am better now after managing the Telugu GLS; and for me, Dr Bobby is the face of his organization. And I resolutely acknowledge Dr Bobby as my teacher, who propelled me into another realm of (Bible) translation work.

Short of stature, but a giant among men, always adorning a courteous air of professionalism, yet always ready to break into a charming smile and come across with a warm-hearted attitude of camaraderie. My only regret is that I couldn't know the man more intimately.

When I think of Dr Bobby Chellappan, I am reminded of the quote, "An intelligent man will open your mind, a handsome man will open your eyes and a gentleman will open your heart." He was handsome, intelligent and a complete and gentle man of God.

K. Job Sudarshan. Ph.D.
Department of Psychology
Andhra Loyola College
Vijayawada
Andhra Pradesh

A few lines of my memory and my association with Rev. Dr. Bobby Chellappan

– R George Edward

It is a great honor to be asked to write a few words about Rev. Dr. Bobby Chellappan, whom I admired very much as a role model to lead a team of the servants of the Lord who were with various background traits. While Bobby was making enormous contributions to the cause of Mission in general and to the cause of Bible Translation Ministry in particular, he maintained his uniqueness in carrying out the task entrusted to him in various ways.

My first work relationship with Bobby just began on the very first day of my association with him on the coldest morning in New Delhi where he came with his beloved wife and Bro. Rinu to pick me up at the New Delhi Airport. He gave me a warm welcome with his style of godly smile and drove the car to the office. On the way, he introduced his wife to me and made a genuine inquiry about my family.

I have witnessed that Bobby was always ready and willing to render pastoral care and concern to his colleagues and subordinates, who used to visit him in the office. Even when he made a quick visit to the Ashram where I sat together with CiTs for consultant checking, I never missed his inquiry about my work and family. As the General Manager of the organization, he proved to be a great source of encouragement and guidance to everybody who worked under his able leadership.

I have also observed Bobby for 5 years and hence I won't hesitate to say that he was one of few Indian Christian leaders who have risen and reclaimed the image in which they have been made! Spending qualitative time with the Master, offering constructive criticism, and smiling hospitality were the hallmarks of Bobby's life and ministry.

Having been armed with various administrative skills, Bobby could handle any sort of issues in ministry or administration both at micro and macro levels. He never failed to claim his right to manhood and dignity. Bobby's greatness consists in his openness and availability to His ministry, expressed in his daring acceptance of any situation with all its challenges. His contribution to the life and ministry of many Bible translators and pastors has been outstanding and unique, and it is a great gift of God.

Bobby rendered strong support to the ongoing varied ministries of their company headed by Cmdr. Thomas Mathew. Being an able administrator, he had a genuine concern about others; as and when any of his colleagues asked him a question or raised an issue, he would start with a gentle smile and half of the answer was already given by then. He had total focus, an attribute that deeply impressed me often.

Bobby was also involved in pastoral ministry in a Church in New Delhi, pastoring, leading, and counseling the congregation with his sound Biblical knowledge and discernment. I had the opportunity to listen to several of his messages delivered in his Church and later posted in media for a wider reach. Undoubtedly, he was a contemplative pastor who maintained a strict devotional bond with his Master.

Bobby also used to teach in a seminary regularly and raised several servants of God for His glory! Several of his students and mentees are now serving the Lord in various parts of this country, many of whom I met with in due course of my ministry in New Delhi, Chhattisgarh, Andhra Pradesh, and Karnataka. It means Bobby has made a huge investment in the lives of many younger generations of the contemporary world.

Bobby has left an impressive legacy, *a legacy that is etched into the minds of others* and lived an exemplary Christian life. His impact-making smile was one of his precious traits and he maintained it till he breathed last. Now Bobby can affirm in the presence of His Master along with the Apostle Paul, "I have fought the good fight, I have finished the race, I have kept the faith." Praise the Lord!

In a nutshell, I can say that Bobby was one of the greatest and noblest of the modern Bible Translation movement in our country, an immense personality, unique, lovable, sublime, and the peerless mission leader of our time. Let me pay a tribute of love and respect to late Bobby, because he used his matchless power for the good of his colleagues, subordinates and above all, various Bibleless people groups of our motherland!

Dr. George Edward
Bible Consultant

"Precious in the sight of the LORD is the death of his saints."

Psalm 116:15 KJV

Dr. Bobby had a great vision for India, and I hope and pray we keep this vision in front of us.

In June of 2019, we began a wonderful friendship with Dr. Bobby and a great partnership with the organization that he was working with to bring the Bible in native languages to India. I visited Bangalore, India, in June of that year to attend the digital bible library summit which was held at Bible Society of India offices to connect with other partners with the shared goal of bringing the light to the Indian nation by providing free and wide access to the Bible.

During the break, I saw Dr. Bobby coming toward my side with a big smile on his face as if he had found a treasure! He introduced himself, introduced the translation work he was busy with at their organization, and asked the question, "Can Davar record our Bibles?". To be honest, at that time I didn't know Dr. Bobby well, I didn't know his work and the translation quality, but I saw a passionate person with a big love for his nation and the courage to bring the Word of God to the Indian nation freely to every person.

Three months later, we signed an agreement and started our partnership with Dr. Bobby and his organization. Through that partnership, Dr. Bobby connected us with Commander Matthew, a very precious brother and friend and the whole organization who serve humbly among the nation of India. During our time with Dr. Bobby, we succeeded to complete recording the gateway languages for India and three years later are still busy with other languages. Dr. Bobby was the key to our great partnership and journey, and I am thankful to Our Lord Jesus for these angels in our lives to bridge our steps toward His Kingdom.

It was a short visit but very rich, my friend Bobby went to be with the Lord on Aug 26, 2021, leaving a clear understanding and preparations for others to continue his legacy to bring the Light, The Word of God to all Indian nation in their heart languages.

From Him and to Him, May His name be Glorified.

Ehab Jabour
CFO| Senior Vice President
Davar Partners International

DR. DAVID REEVE'S THOUGHTS ABOUT DR. BOBBY

Transcript from January 17, 2022, unfolding Word All-Staff Meeting in Orlando, Florida.

As I look back over the past eleven years, I am stunned at what God has done in my own life; the healing that has taken place. The profound opportunities that came about as I continued to look for and walk with Him. I've been profoundly touched by people who have come into and out of my life, who have come alongside me and been a blessing. One of those people was Dr. Bobby.

Last January, Dr. Bobby was here in the room with us (at the January 2021 Unfolding Word All-Staff Conference). (See photo with Russ Perry. See also group photo).

Dr. Bobby had a profound influence on our work in India. He was very effective as a pastor and evangelist there in India. When I first started talking to him, he told me that God had laid something on his heart, "I've got something bigger for you." Dr. Bobby thought, what in the world could be bigger than what I am already doing, Lord? How can that be?

Not long after that, our friend, Commander Matthew, from India, reached out to him and said, "I need your help with a strategy to reach all the gateway languages in India."

When he heard Commander Matthew describing what he wanted him to do, Dr. Bobby immediately understood that this was God's direction for him. Working on the Gateway Languages strategy for all of India was something much bigger than he had ever imagined. Dr. Bobby's work with the gateway languages in India was highly effective. I have more than a dozen letters from various Church denominational leaders thanking us for allowing them to be part of the gateway language strategy that Dr. Bobby helped implement there.

From late 2019 to early 2020, Dr. Bobby again sensed the Lord saying, "I have something else for you. Something bigger." Dr. Bobby wondered what that could be, but he was a man of faith willing to do whatever God told him to do. So, he began exploring what it might mean to work with Unfolding Word. We talked about the idea of him coming on board the Unfolding Word team and helping us work globally to implement what he had already done in India. Take the same experience and do it in Africa, in the Middle East, and around the world.

He was such a successful pastor and an effective communicator. I was looking forward to having him on our team and by my side, leading the Church-Centric Bible Translation movement.

Last January, Dr. Bobby came to our All-Staff meeting. He also went to our Church-Centric Bible Translation Intensive training that followed. Immediately after that, we boarded a plane bound for Grand Rapids, Michigan, where a film studio recorded several hours of video material with us. The video was in preparation for his work with Unfolding Word, leading the CCBT strategy with global Church networks.

(See Dr. Bobby's video).

Our friend, Dr. Bobby, has gone to be with Jesus now. He got called up to be something greater. I'm sure that shortly after he walked through the Pearly Gates, he got involved in doing something more significant than he had ever imagined. The Lord indeed had something greater for him to do.

Men like Dr. Bobby inspire me to keep pressing ahead.

The Lord is doing something profound. We're players in His epic story. If you haven't paid attention to that, please do. Don't listen to what the world has to say. The Lord continues to write His grand story, and like Dr. Bobby, you and I are part of it.

"See, I am doing a new thing!

Now it springs up; do you not perceive it?

I am making a way in the wilderness

and streams in the wasteland."

– **Isaiah 43:19**

Dr. David Reeves
Unfolding Word
USA

I first met Dr. Bobby in February 2016 when I visited him for a Gateway Language Bible translation project meeting. He immediately impressed me as competent and confident, but also a gracious and humble man of God. I got to know Dr. Bobby more in the following months and years as we worked closely together on the Bible translation project. He was serious, passionate, and diligent about the work of Bible translation. But he was also full of joy and quick to smile. When we discussed the details of a project, Dr. Bobby would first patiently listen to understand. Then after absorbing and analyzing the discussion, I could always count on him to gently share his thoughts and wisdom that never failed to put the project on a better track toward success. Some of my fondest memories were the times I stayed at the Classic Diplomat Hotel near the airport in Delhi, and Dr. Bobby and Jobby would pick me up in the mornings to take me to the office and deliver me back to the hotel in the evenings. We would spend the time in the car chatting about all kinds of topics, but Dr Bobby never talked about himself until one day at the office, when we finished meetings early, I asked him to tell me his story. I was amazed at Dr. Bobby's testimony of the way God worked miracles in his family and how he came to faith in Christ, and then all that God enabled Dr. Bobby to do in ministry.

However, in his typical humble way, Dr. Bobby was quick to give all the praise and glory to God for the grace He showed in his life. My last opportunity to spend time with Dr. Bobby in person was when he paid a visit to Orlando, FL in January, and February of 2021 for meetings with unfolding Word. We usually walked together back and forth from the hotel to the meeting venue, and I enjoyed the casual conversations we had. He also shared stories and laughter with our group in the evenings when had dinner together. I am blessed to have known Dr. Bobby and to have been able to call him my friend, as well as a brother in Christ. I will miss him greatly as a friend, and the joy of working alongside him as a fellow servant in the Kingdom of God. I just listened again to the audio of an interview one of my colleagues did with Dr. Bobby in March 2020, and when asked about the urgency of the Bible translation task, Dr. Bobby had this to say: The time is short, and things all around the country are not going the way it should be. This is the gap that we have right now, where we can push things and make it happen right now in our times, in our generation. And I believe God is giving us this opportunity still. It's a time when the Church can come together and put all its force to move forward and get this work accomplished. I believe as of now the doors of India are still open, despite the persecutions. Churches are coming up everywhere. Even though the statistics may not declare it, when you go to the field, you see there are churches that never existed before. In almost all language groups, there are churches there. But they do not have the resources. The danger is, one, that because they do not have Bibles or study materials, they are not equipped, strengthened and rooted. So, the danger is that the places they came from, and the backgrounds they came from, can easily divert them back and take them away. Secondly, wrong teachings can easily influence them, and they can deviate from the original calling in their lives. So, it's important to get the word of God to them and the resources. We can train disciples and equip them to be grounded, rooted and strong so that they can be kingdom builders and through them the vast population needs to be touched. So that's very important to be done right away.

Russ Perry
Unfolding Word
USA

INSPIRED BY BOBBY'S OBEDIENCE

January 2021 was a moment of crisis for me. I had been struggling for several months, almost a year, with a decision that would radically alter the course of my life. After 32 years serving as a pastor with the last 24 at Faith Community Church in Virginia, it seemed that God was leading me to leave the Church and work as a full-time writer with Unfolding Word.

In one sense, this leading was the culmination of a dream. God led me to start a writing ministry in 2002. I did not know where or how he would use it, but I knew that was the path. Between 2005 and 2013, I wrote two books for JAARS, an aviation and technical support arm of Wycliffe Bible Translators. I wrote a weekly blog for ten years, several articles for our local newspaper, and volunteered for Unfolding Word for three years. But finding a new pastor is difficult for any church. Stress fractures can appear, and problems can multiply. I was deeply attached to the people of Faith Community Church (FCC). My attempts to mentor two other young men into that role as FCC's pastor had not worked out. I was worried about what might happen to the Church if I left.

That's when I met Dr. Bobby Chellappan. He was in Orlando, Florida, for Unfolding Word's semi-annual All Staff conference. My friend and the CEO of Unfolding Word, David Reeves, recommended that I get to know Bobby. So, on January 26, 2021, we sat together for lunch.

You must understand that pastors are a different breed. Our shepherding and leadership responsibilities make our life experiences unlike most people's. So, it is always encouraging to sit down with a brother pastor. I was looking forward to sharing with Dr. Bobby as a brother pastor and learning from his leadership experiences. I did not realize how convicting our visit would be!

After sharing a little bit of my background and story, I asked Dr. Bobby about his. The outline of his life went something like this.

As a young man, he became a thriving tourist industry executive in Delhi. His father, who was retired from the Air Force, had planted and led a healthy church. The Church asked Bobby to take over when his father's health failed. Soon, however, many elders left because of no confidence in a younger man. The Church declined from 300 (not sure about this number) to 10. There was a money crisis. But Bobby trusted God and was doing both jobs, pastor, and tourist industry executive, for a while. Then, the Church grew. He became the first TV evangelist in Delhi, played a part in a movie about the faith, and became a professor at Grace Bible Seminary.

At this point, Dr. Bobby's ministry was going very well. Then one day, God spoke to him, saying, "I'm going to move you into a greater sphere of ministry."

Now here's the thing that convicted me so profoundly. Dr. Bobby immediately obeyed. Commander Thomas Matthew, realizing the scope of the Gateway Language Bible Translation project, said, "We need Bobby." When they called, Bobby answered. He was not afraid to leave the successful Church ministry and all the other things he was doing. He believed those things belonged to God, not him, and that God would take care of them. They called him to manage the whole GL project for Operation Agape through Bridge Connectivity Solutions. He just obeyed and didn't worry about it.

When he finished the GL project, he obeyed God again. Having completed that Gateway Language translation task, God again interrupted and told Bobby, "I am moving you into a larger sphere of ministry." That's when David Reeves contacted him and said, "Dr. Bobby, I believe God has a role for you in the global Church-Centric Bible Translation movement. Will you come to work with us?"

Again, without hesitating, Dr. Bobby obeyed. That's why he was at the Unfolding Word All Staff Conference that day because when God called, he obeyed.

We finished lunch, took our trays to the kitchen, shook hands, and went our separate ways. My responsibilities at the conference kept me up late that night. I fell into bed without thinking too much about it. The following day, I skipped the early sessions and stayed in my hotel room thinking about Dr. Bobby's obedience and praying. When I finished, I went to the conference center, found my friend David Reeves, and said, "OK, I'm ready."

I resigned from Faith Community Church and went to work full-time with Unfolding Word on August 1.

Dr. Bobby's death came as a profound shock to all of us. I grieved that I would never get to know this brother better and share this great faith adventure called Unfolding Word with him. But his legacy lives on in every life inspired by his obedience.

Dane Skelton
Unfolding Word
USA

ASSOCIATES

Pastor Bobby – A Tribute

Occasionally you come across a person who leaves a profound and deep impact on your life; for me, Pastor Bobby was certainly one of those people. He not only inspired, influenced, and impacted me, but countless others, who have had the privilege of meeting and knowing him.

I shall always remember Pastor Bobby for his humility, and his gentle, respectful, passionate disposition; a true mark of being a mighty man of God. I have had the honor and privilege of knowing Pastor Bobby since 2007, and we have since then, shared special times in ministry together.

At the heart of Pastor Bobby's ministry was his deep conviction, commitment and passion for the Gospel, and his commitment to spreading this Good News around the world. He shared the Gospel in his inimitable style- simple, yet powerful. He was intentional to stay immersed and saturated in the Word of God. Pastor Bobby will always be remembered as a highly accomplished, gifted communicator, who had a genuine interest in everyone and everything, while ever smiling. As I reflect on Pastor Bobby, his life was his message…a simple man, who had responded to God's love, by placing his faith in Jesus. He was on fire for Christ, and the flames that burned in his heart for the lost were contagious.

The friendship I have shared with Pastor Bobby and his wife, Blessy, has been a great source of encouragement and strength to me. I have immense respect for Blessy. She is the epitome of a Proverbs 31 wife, who has stood tall and strong beside her husband, in every situation. The grace, strength, dignity, and elegance with which she conducts herself speak volumes about her. I have been inspired by her steadfast faith in her savior and maker, the Lord Jesus Christ, during her grief and loss. I truly believe that the Lord has anointed, and appointed Blessy, to carry on the good work and legacy of Pastor Bobby. Being confident of this very thing: that He who has begun a good work will perform it until the day of Jesus Christ.

While none of us have answers for his early home-going, we trust the Lord. Even though life without Pastor Bobby will never be the same, it is the Lord's hope and assurance that keep us strong. We believe that surely goodness and mercy shall follow Blessy and the children, all the days of their lives. May the Lord teach us to number our days, that we may apply our hearts unto wisdom.

"Our consolation is that Pastor Bobby lived an impactful life, raising men and women across the globe for Jesus." Pastor Bobby's life can be summed up in the words of the Apostle Paul, "I have fought a good fight, I have finished my course, I have kept the faith." We celebrate, cherish and honor Pastor Bobby, a General in the faith, for his life and legacy, which will forever be cherished.

Rev. Minny Lal
Associate Minister
Morris Cerullo Ministries

Our memory of meeting Bobby for the first time goes back to the year 1994 in a youth meeting where he, as a vibrant preacher, brought the Word with great courage and passion. The call of God to be a teacher and preacher of the Word was very clear in his life. Bobby truly was a vessel in the hands of God and a gift to the body of Christ.

His love and zeal for His Master stood out in his life. His burning desire to see a transformation drew him to the presence of God to seek His face with fasting and prayer. He was involved in city-wide and nationwide prayer gatherings.

We have seen him blooming in his career and ministry. His commitment to God and his career was well balanced.

His devotion and dedication to God and his parents were noteworthy. He was an affectionate son to his parents. The way Bobby cared for his dad during his physically challenged years was commendable.

The first time he visited us personally was to invite us to his wedding. God blessed him with a suitable life partner Blessy who shared his vision and burden standing shoulder to shoulder with him till the end.

God brought him to various positions and leadership by broadening his vision. His burning desire to see a transformation in the nation was commendable. He always showed great honor towards servants of God.

We last met Bobby in our home a couple of months before he went to be with the Lord. He had come with Blessy and the children to spend some time with us after ministering in a Mission Training Retreat organized by their church- Apostolic Faith Church on our premises. That day he shared with us their vision and plans. Before leaving he humbly asked both of us to pray for him and the family by laying our hands on them. Little did we know that it was our last meeting on this side of the shore.

He kept the faith, finished his race and is waiting for his crown from the master's hands.

In summary, his was a life short-lived, well spent for Jesus Christ our lord.

Dr. Josh & Dinu Kalliimel
Abundant Life Church
New Delhi

Loving Memory of Bro Bobby Chellappan

Greetings in Jesus's Name! I'm Bishop Dr. Sudhir Kavuri from Canada General Overseer of the Global Christian Network

Writing this in the loving memory of our dear beloved apostle and dear brother Bobby Chellappan-

When I recollect my association with him, it was in 2010 when I moved to Delhi/Noida from South India, Andhra Pradesh.

As I was doing Gospel Ministry there, it was in the Fire Conference in Haryana. On the last day of the Conference, I was so depressed and concerned about my future that time. Brother Bobby laid his hand on me and prayed. I still remember, he said "Lord, strengthen him!" Immediately my mind was cleared, and I felt great peace and strength in my heart. I received the touch of the Lord and from that day onwards the Lord strengthened me.

I understood and have seen from that time his passion, I may say God's Compassion in him and from him as a Leader and the Lord honored his Word by answering his prayer as an apostle's authority and from that time, I had due respect for him.

Later we met at a couple of conferences at Siloam Global Worship Center, and in other national conferences in New Delhi and a couple of times, I visited his church.

In 2012, I moved back to South India and from there went to the USA and was there till 2017 in USA. So, I used to be in touch with him online on Facebook and on WhatsApp.

When I came back to India in 2017, he invited me to his Church to share the word, so I did and shared the word and met him and his dear wife and congregation.

Later I moved to Canada in 2019 July, and I was in touch with him on WhatsApp through the Global Christian Network. He was actively involved in a few Global Networks, and I was able to introduce him to other Global Ministries where he shared the word online due to Corona.

In 2019 December he visited Canada and came to Vancouver. So, I was able to meet him. I didn't know that was the last time I would see him – a very humble man of God and loving and compassionate. His presence is a great loss here, but I'm sure he is with the Lord in a better place.

When he came to Canada, he texted me that he was in a hotel near the airport Vancouver. So, I went and met him in the hotel with some Indian sweets that my wife had prepared for him. He was very happy and said to convey my greetings to my sister. I took him out to explore a few places here in Vancouver and I remember we went to McDonald's for dinner. I was about to pay but my credit card did not work. So, he paid for both of us, and we took some pictures together. He shared his ministry activities and what the Lord was doing, and he gave me a Christian Movie CD that he had acted in.

And lastly, he said that he was making plans to settle in the USA with his family. I said to him that I would offer him my full support to help him settle there and inform him and introduce him to a few people there in the USA; though of course, he had many good connections in the USA, Canada, and all over the world.

After he reached India, we communicated through WhatsApp, and he did reply every time immediately after he checked my messages. We shared each other's prayer requests and he used to encourage me. Then on 2021 August 15, I sent my birthday pictures and informed him to receive blessings from him as usual on WhatsApp. But I didn't get any reply from him, and I thought he was busy or changed his phone number. Later this year in January, I heard from one pastor in the UK, that he passed away in 2021 August and I was shocked and couldn't believe it. Later I was able to learn from his Church members and his dear wife too of his sudden demise.

He was very Passionate about his Ministry and was humble, apart from being a good brother and friend and also very responsible to his family as a son to his mom and dad, a good husband to his wife, good father to his children, a loving brother and good friend to all of us. He had a very good name in the Christian community in New Delhi and other parts of the world and in the nation of India.

Thank you, Bro. Bobby, for what you imparted into my life. Miss you bro and the Christian world misses you very much. I'm sure you are with the Lord and in a better place. Also, I believe you finished the course and I'm sure the Lord said – "Good and Faithful servant, Enter into my Joy!"

And I wish and my prayers for his beloved wife and children and Church is that - what he did leave a legacy that will continue till Jesus Comes to see India and Delhi saved and Revival in India.

Bishop Dr. Sudhir Kavuri D. Th, D. Min, D.Div

General Overseer of Global Christian Network

Canada

Phone No/WhatsApp: +1 604-206-5559

Email: sudhirkavuri@yahoo.com

Twitter: @GCN180

REFLECTIONS

NEED FOR BIBLE TRAINING

– Bishop Dr. John Joseph

Act 6:7- And the word of God increased; and the number of the disciples multiplied in Jerusalem greatly; and a great company of the priests were obedient to the faith.

Until Acts Chapter Six, the Bible repeatedly mentions that the number of believers multiplied. Many were baptized and filled with the Holy Spirit. But Acts Chapter Six and Verse Seven mention that "The number of disciples multiplied greatly…."

We know there is a difference between a believer and a disciple. A believer is one who believes in what Jesus did on the cross, buried and rose again on the third day. But a disciple is one who puts into practice all that he believes.

The dictionary meaning of the word 'disciple' is a follower or a student.

The word Disciples or Discipleship has been mentioned 257 times in the New Testament!

I believe these are two major levels of every Christian – 1. Believer. 2. Disciple.

The Great Commission which Jesus commanded us to do involved raising more disciples "…. Mat 28:20. Teaching them to observe all things whatsoever I have commanded you:"

We know the difference between preaching and teaching. Jesus wanted us not only to preach the gospel but also to change their way of life by teaching the correct principles.

Pastor Bobby Chellappan was very passionate about raising disciples. When the option of starting a part-time Bible school came forward through Life Christian University (India), he immediately liked the idea and started it in his church. He raised and trained many in the Word of God. He was a strong visionary who had foresight as to what was coming next and planned accordingly. His passion for raising disciples was unparalleled and unmatched. I am glad that now his wife Blessy has taken up that passion and is involved in the same ministry as her husband.

Remember: All living things grow!

One of the characteristics of living things is that they grow.

It is a sign of life.

They are called to grow.

They are designed to grow.

They not only grow but multiply and thrive.

(Remember: Dead things don't grow nor multiply)

A Church is a Living Organism.

It must grow.

It must multiply.

It must thrive.

It must bear fruits.

(Remember: Dead things don't grow nor multiply nor thrive_

All parts of a tree, including its roots, trunk, and everything else must function well so that one day branches will perform their duty of bearing many fruits. Likewise, a church!

Jesus once said:

Mat 4:19 - And He said to them, Follow Me, and I will make you fishers of men.

Right from the beginning of His ministry, Jesus was interested in making disciples.

Now fishing is an art. It requires skill and talent. Not everyone can fish. I once tried my luck at fishing, and it turned out to be a disaster! (I ended up killing the fish I caught!!!). It was a messy job – gathering earthworms, fixing them on the hook, catching the fish and then unhooking the fish – it all requires some training. It also requires patience. That day I caught hold of my ears and said I will never do it again!

In Luke 5:4-11, Jesus once gave his disciples a "fishing experience" which they had never witnessed before. There is a 'carpenter' giving a fishing lesson to fishermen. (It may sound very strange, but He did a better job!) Therefore, Peter reacted, "We have fished all night and caught nothing". Peter is trying to tell this 'carpenter' that this is not the time to fish. All fishermen know that the net is cast at night and pulled back in the morning. But Jesus is explaining that cast your nets according to His word and His timing. It goes to prove that soul-winning will be accomplished not according to our wisdom, experience, talents, and strengths but according to His word!

Jesus also said: Mat 9:37-38 -Then He said to His disciples, the harvest truly is plenteous, but the laborers are few. (38) Therefore, pray to the Lord of the harvest that He will send out laborers into His harvest.

Jesus is talking about sending laborers. We only send those who are trained, experienced and skillful in their trade. In fact, in every industry, there are two types of workers: skilled and unskilled.

The unskilled worker works the same number of hours but can be easily replaced by another or even fired! The skilled type of worker is hard to find. He sits in a white-collar job with all the best amenities and is paid a much bigger salary!!!

Jesus was very interested in training His disciples. He wanted trained, experienced, and skillful workers. The Bible says:

(Luke 10:1) After these things the Lord appointed other seventy also and sent them two by two before his face into every city and place, whither he would come.

What was the need to appoint 70 more disciples? Were the 12 not sufficient? Jesus knew the need of the hour. When He said the harvest is plenteous, He was mindful of the need of workers to reap the harvest. Many times we do believe that the harvest is plenteous, but we are not acting or preparing to reap the harvest. Jesus knew he would need more talented, anointed, skillful servants of God. He was always mindful to train more disciples like Himself. Even right from the very beginning of his ministry, he was mindful to raise disciples. In Mat. 4:19, he called Peter and Andrew, then James and John and others. He started this process of recruiting new disciples very soon. According to Mathew, the first sermon that Jesus preached was "Repent: for the kingdom of heaven is at hand" Mat 4:17 and immediately following that He was found calling out men into ministry. (Mat 4:19).

I believe the Church today should focus on these two major issues: 1. Evangelism and 2. Discipleship. We must save souls and then train them into disciples to win more souls.

The Great Commission included Evangelism and Discipleship – Mat 28:19. Paul wrote in Romans 10:13 … whosoever will call on the name of the Lord shall be saved. But how shall they call … unless believe …. Hear …. Preach …. Sent. So, this is a complete cycle of the Kingdom of God. 1. Sent 2. Preach 3. Hear 4. Believe 5. Call 6. Saved. This is a system that God ordained in the Kingdom of God for it to grow.

Just imagine Jesus in his short period of 3 ½ years trained 82 disciples! If Jesus had to live 80 years (the least that you and I expect) then at this rate, he would have raised at least 1148 disciples! We must take this issue seriously. I have always said this: "A Church is not known by the number of members it has but by the number of disciples it has."

Moses in his lifetime raised 70 disciples. (Numbers 11:16)

Elijah had a school of prophets and later took over the school with a greater anointing. (2 Kings 2:3)

Peter and the apostles were having a Bible school therefore Acts 6:7 it says that the number of disciples multiplied greatly in Jerusalem.

The Church today must be most involved in Discipleship and Raising New Leaders.

Now there are very good full-time Bible colleges in our country offering various Bible degrees. People who have got a calling for full time ministry should go to such universities. But what about those who want to be involved in ministry but missed the opportunity to earn a Bible University Degree? Where will they go? Life Christian University (India) (LCU) comes to their rescue and offers part-time Bible programmes which will enable them to be involved in the ministry. Now with an online facility, it is much easier to earn a Bible College degree.

I believe God is in command and is aware of the present-day situations. He was bold enough to declare (Mat 16:18): I will build my Church and the gates of hell shall not prevail against it.

Be encouraged. Be bold. Be strong for God is building His church!!!

Bishop Dr. John Joseph
Director, Life Christian University
Maharashtra

Mission as Establishing the Kingdom of God

– Rev. Dr. Joseph Mathew

The intrinsic connection between mission and the Kingdom of God is a proven truth to which the Bible attests significantly. The mission unfolds the Kingdom, and the Kingdom fulfills the mission. I am glad to reflect on the foundational concepts of mission and the Kingdom as this Festschrift of Bobby Chellappan is posthumously published. This paper explores the dynamics of Mission in establishing the Kingdom of God as we remember the life and contribution of the servant of God who left a legacy.

Defining Mission

The definition of mission is multifaceted, and the word must be understood from various dimensions such as Biblical, historical, theological, and contextual perspectives. Here are some of the attempts to define the mission. The book Introducing World Missions: A Biblical, Historical and Practical Survey jointly authored by Scott A. Moreau, Gray R Corwin and Gary B. McGee defines that 'Mission is like an unexplored cave". Exploration of caves meets with dark tunnels, twists, and turns. So is mission. It is interesting to note that the mission goes through unexpected turns and twists as the context demands. This is true when we consider that "Mission has been relegated to the specific work of the Church and agencies in the task of reaching people for Christ by crossing cultural boundaries" (p.17). In a broader sense mission refers to everything the Church is doing proclaiming the Kingdom of God. Timothy Nyasulu, an African mission theologian points to the features of mission in the following way:

1. Witnessing to the Kingdom. Jesus announced the Kingdom of God and commanded His disciples to be his witnesses. (Acts. 1:8)
2. It is the propagation of salvation, calling to repentance, conversion, and faith in Christ. Christ gives forgiveness and salvation.
3. Conscious attempt to propagate Christian faith.
4. Also, can be treated as an effecting influence.

Mission pertains to the message of God's Kingdom made known in Jesus Christ, as intended for all nations. Nyasulu attempts to understand mission as the dynamic relationship between God and the world. God sends Himself, His Son, and His church. Those who are actively involved in the vision of His redemptive will understand themselves as "sent" individuals or groups. Therefore, Mission cannot be defined in a restricted sense.

Kingdom of God

The theme of the Kingdom of God is central to the understanding of the process and promise of the mission. The Kingdom of God occupies the central place in the "Missio Dei".

One of the books that describe the dynamics of the Kingdom is *Mission as Transformation: A Theology of the Whole Gospel edited by Vinay Samuel and Chris Sugden. This book* is a collection of writings and reports, that present the Kingdom of God as the pivotal force of the mission. The biblical foundation of the Kingdom of God lies in the fact that God is the King above all gods as Creator, Sustainer, Owner, and Ruler. God handed over the stewardship of creation to human beings and ushers everyone who repent into the Kingdom. Jesus, while preaching the Kingdom challenged the evils of the society. When he atoned for the sin on the Cross, Kingdom became the abode of the forgiven sinners.

King and the Kingdom are inseparable. Kingdom becomes evident where His people profess the King. Where people do His will, signs of the Kingdom emerge in society. God enabled Jesus Christ through the Holy Spirit to demonstrate the Kingdom. Church is to be the visible expression of the Kingdom. The signs of the Kingdom are: 1) the Presence of Jesus; 2) Proclamation of the Gospel; 3) Conversion and new birth; 4) Church and Mission; 5) Deliverance from the forces of sin; 6) Holy Spirit in power; 7) Fruit of the Holy Spirit; and 8) A courageous bearing of suffering for righteousness.

The Church is established by Jesus to witness to the Kingdom. Church as the body of Christ is the visible evidence of the Kingdom of God. Servanthood is the primary qualification of the Kingdom. God delegates authority to men and women to establish His Kingdom upon the earth. The fallen principalities pose a challenge and are in enmity to the Kingdom. All Kingdom ministry is an implicit or explicit call to discipleship. Dynamics of the Kingdom is found in the gift of the Spirit as the mark of new creation. At baptism, Jesus became the bearer of the Spirit, whereas in Pentecost he became the giver of the Spirit. The gifts of the Spirit are given in ministries for building up the church, to be experienced as a release of God's effective power in the ministry of the Kingdom in the world.

The Kingdom of God functions in polarities, such as present and future, individual and social, spirit and matter, gradual and climatic, divine action and human action, and Church and the kingdom. Such polarities give us a more realistic understanding of the Kingdom. For example, the already-but-not-yet tension should protect us from triumphalism and pessimism.

As far as the Kingdom and ethics are concerned, the ethical teaching of Jesus is important. The Sermon on the Mount depicts "repentance" and "righteousness" belonging to the Kingdom. The ethics of Jesus have to be practiced as the behavioral expression of God's over-mastering rule in behavior and church.

Vinay Samuel and Sugaden present the Kingdom of God as the paradigmatic agent of transformation. Kingdom of God as the over-arching theme of the Bible gives the basis, content, and direction of the mission. There are eight distinctive components of transformation listed in the book: 1. Integral relation between evangelism and social change. 2. Mission as a journey and witness with the world not as a judgement made from outside. 3. Making faith addressing the context. 4. Praxis, not neutrality, geared to probe results is what the Kingdom prescribes. 5. Context is local, that is to say, micro reality is taken into serious consideration. 6. Stresses on the liberating and empowering dimension of the gospel. 7. Reconciliation and solidarity are key concerns and 8. Building up communities of change marks the function of the Kingdom ministry.

Arthur F. Glasser in The Story of God's Mission in the Bible: Announcing the Kingdom puts forth a different view on the Kingdom of God. Glasser mostly makes a biblical, theological, and historical survey to identify the golden thread of the mission theme of God's Kingdom. The book presents the Kingdom of God as the connecting theme of mission based on the premise that the whole Bible is a book of mission, the story of God's revelation. In the Old Testament God's rule is given the centrality. The way the argument is built in the book is very interesting which eventually leads to the centrality of the Kingdom in the New Testament all the way to the consummation of the purpose of God. Glasser presents seven axioms pertinent to the theme of mission in the Old Testament. 1. God, who is righteous and just, is sovereign in his rule. 2). God's sovereign rule demands personal commitment. God is not fascinated by mere external rituals but by a sheer commitment to his interest and character (Micah 6:8). 3). God's subjects must constitute a "servant" community. That means a spirit of service and openness must be the distinguishing mark of God's servants. 4). The Old Testament community of the King becomes the New Testament body of Christ. 5). God's people are called to Mission. Because the sovereignty of God's rule needs to be established over all creation. 6). God's sovereign rule will be resisted and opposed by the people-- by the nations-- that do not know him, and by the unseen powers. 7). The direction of God's rule is always into the future.

In the New Testament, according to Glasser, the Kingdom of God occupies the centrality of Jesus' ministry. Jesus inaugurated the Kingdom and taught the present, future, and the ethical commitment of the Kingdom through parables and exhortations, for example, in the teaching of the Sermon on the Mount. Jesus identified himself as the servant of God and worker of miracles, demonstrating the power and authority of the Kingdom. He fulfilled the Old Testament Kingdom roles of priest, prophet, servant, and king in his earthly ministry. Also, Jesus announced the Kingdom and its blessings for the Gentiles. One best example is that he declared the temple to be the house of prayer for the Gentiles at the temple cleansing event. At Pentecost, the Church was equipped with the power of the Spirit to minister as a Kingdom people. The apostles witnessed to and ministered on the Kingdom principles. The Book of Revelation brings the finality and consummation of God's purpose and plan for history and creation, establishing God's rule forever.

The Kingdom is multi-dimensional in its constitution and application. Jesus compared the Kingdom of God to the leaven (Matthew 13: 33) which transforms the whole flour. One can use this metaphor to make clear the interrelatedness of the above arguments about the Kingdom, and how it builds coherence. Glasser's argument can be seen as the gradual emergence of the Kingdom (leaven) progressively revealed and emerging, and finally changing the whole lump. Whereas Vinay Samuel throws light on the actual process of the transformation, of leaven leavening the lump, and the result. However, both views throw light on different areas of the Kingdom and contribute to configuring the total picture.

Kingdom and Mission in India

The need to accomplish the transformational aspect of the mission with the centrality of the Kingdom is very important to the Indian context. India invites the gospel to transform its social, cultural, religious, and economic fabric. The caste system is an evil that needs to be transformed to establish more egalitarian society. Cultural hegemony must be deconstructed to ensure the preservation of all cultures and to safeguard the co-existence of cultures. Economic disparity must be established because the Kingdom perceives justice.

The emphasis on the aspects of the Kingdom discussed in the above two books has a greater relevance to the context of India. The integral relation between evangelism and social change defines our direction of mission in India. Evangelism without social engagement remains ineffective and fruitless. Also, it is important that the

Mission as a journey witness the realities of India not as a judgement made from outside is important. God has a special plan for India and that is to deliver this country in all aspects of its life. It is highly important to make faith addressing the context. The context of India is multi-pronged. The cultural, linguistic, and ethnic diversity is a challenge as well as an opportunity in mission. Breaking the strongholds of each culture and the people group is a huge task that needs to be done with utmost care and divine power. Each culture must get the best as God intended them to be.

Praxis, not neutrality, is what the mission in India demands. Mere propagation and campaigns won't be enough. Mission anywhere demands engagement in life. That's what Jesus did by healing the sick, feeding the hungry, giving sight to the blind and raising the dead. Praxis is action-reflection geared to probe results, and that is what the Kingdom prescribes. Praxis requires a proper understanding of the context. One must bear in mind that context is local, micro reality is taken into serious consideration. The Mission must be relevant to the context in practice and the method. Of course, the context of India is vast and complex. Therefore, understanding and engaging with the micro realities of each situation is important. Pandita Ramabai did that when she engaged in fighting the famine of Maharashtra during her time and rehabilitation famine-stricken families, thus making the Mukti Mission relevant to the context of that time.

Paying special attention to the liberating and empowering dimension of the gospel is also very important in the mission in India. Economic liberation is very important like that of spiritual deliverance. Empowering of the weak communities is part of the impact of the gospel. Along with these aspects are reconciliation and solidarity as the key concerns. Solidarity with the poor and the needy is important. Reconciliation of the divided communities and hostile groups needs to be accomplished through the reconciling power of the cross, which is at the centre of the gospel of Jesus Christ. Thus, building up communities of change marks the function of the Kingdom ministry. These concerns have paramount importance to the mission in India.

Having said the above factors about the transformational aspect of the mission and the centrality of the Kingdom concerns in mission, I would like to reflect briefly on the contributions of Dr. Bobby Chellappan. I will look at how he lived the Kingdom's concerns of mission in and through his life and ministry.

Contributions of Dr.Bobby Chellappan

I deem it a great privilege to have been asked to write a paper for the Festschrift on Dr. Bobby's contributions. My association with him was short. I met him for the first time in Delhi when his church, the Apostolic Faith Church hosted one of our National Prayer Meet in 2017. Ever since Dr. Bobby had been a close friend of Light the World Missions.

Dr. Bobby was involved in different areas of ministry in India after giving up his job as a travel consultant such as pastoring, Church planting, teaching, and media ministry. He engaged in teaching at the Life Christian University and served as the Dean of Grace Bible College. He, along with his wife Blessy Bobby ministered on FETV for a year from 2009-10. This channel reached out to 120 countries. Dr. Bobby also ministered on Zee Jagran in prime time for about 6 months while this channel had mainly religious gurus as speakers. Interestingly, he played a key role in a Christian Hindi Movie- 'Rupantar' which is used as a tool for evangelism.

Dr. Bobby organized and was involved in several Mission trips to encourage pastors and leaders in India and abroad. The Mission trip is important as it opens our eyes to the realities on the field and help to cast the vision and to catch the burden for the land. Recent studies show that short-term mission trips are bringing more results.

Bible translation was the highlight of Dr. Bobby's contribution to the Kingdom. He is credited with the efforts in revising the Bible into 12 major gateway languages and setting up processes to get it translated into Indian minority languages. That is a major achievement in the Bible translation ministry. Minority languages are often neglected or paid the least attention. But, when the minority languages are considered for Bible translation, it empowers the communities at the micro level and gets the Word of God rooted into the local culture. Another significant contribution of Dr. Bobby is facilitating the translation of the Bible into the Indian Sign language for the deaf community. That is a great landmark. It is the fulfillment of the Scripture that "In that day the deaf will hear the words of the scroll, and out of gloom and darkness the eyes of the blind will see" (Is. 29: 18), and "Then will the eyes of the blind be opened and the ears of the deaf unstopped" (Is. 35: 5).

While the translation ministry of Dr. Bobby bore fruits in aiding the translation of Christian literature to Indian languages, his ministry also touched other fields such as setting up studios for audio and video recording. He was gifted in media activities as an innovator. Other fields of his ministry extended to organizing pastors' fellowship and supporting missions. Besides, he was a man of 'mission in the marketplaces.' Dr. Bobby was involved in evangelism-both at the personal as well as group level-, street preaching, conducting outreaches in parks, and marketplaces in villages and cities. On the whole, he was deeply committed to the furtherance of mission and thereby establishing the Kingdom through his talents and gifts.

Conclusion

'Biography is the footprint of a person walked on history'. This quote proves its relevance as I conclude this paper by reflecting on the legendary contribution of Dr. Bobby Chellappan. He labored faithfully to fulfil the calling upon his life about the mission and the Kingdom of God. His life and legacy marked transformation. That is, his ministry evoked spiritual and social transformation, and for that, he used the most powerful weapon, the Bible. He did it with the aid of the most impactful forces such as that of media, micro-level empowering, methods of teaching, and initiatives of leadership. His legacy will continue to influence and inspire many like the way Joseph's bones continued to instil hope to the People of God!

****

Rev. Dr. Joseph Mathew
President and Director
Light the World Missions

At Apostolic Faith Church after a National prayer meet conducted by 'Light the World Missions'.

'GOD Whom Bobby Served- Economic Oriented Leadership'.

Introduction

This book is about celebrating the life of Dr Bobby Chellappan. (Let me call him just Bobby here. He was my friend and colleague) This is also about how Bobby handled business, especially finances and the lessons he gave to his company and the team. So, this is about money and wealth. Bobby was managing Bible translation work in several languages. Bible was dear to him. He preached from the Bible, taught the Bible, and lived according to the Bible. Therefore, his handling of finances and money was also fully as per the Bible.

Money and Wealth

We all need money to live in this world. So, what does the Bible teach about money and wealth? Many Christians consider that having money is against Biblical principles. Is that true? When God called and blessed Abraham and many others, He blessed them with material blessings as well. Abraham's descendants – Israel – were given the land, as part of the blessing. However, the Lord reminded them in Lev. 25:23 "The land is Mine", meaning all land and all the wealth belongs to the Lord. Cattle on a thousand hills and wealth in every mine is His. However, remember that the primary blessing was to be God's representatives on this earth – "A kingdom of priests and a holy nation". In this brief chapter, we will not be going into the details, but will be laying down a few basic principles from the Bible that we learned through Bobby. These, I believe, will apply to those who are business leaders, trying to increase profits, or even an ordinary person, struggling to meet his/her ends meet. This will equally apply to leaders who run development organizations or ministry leaders.

John Wesley is reported to have preached "Earn all you can, save all you can, and give all you can". That is a good principle for the disciples of Jesus Christ to follow.

What does the Bible teach us about money?

Stewardship of money

The Bible reminds us again and again that the material possessions that we are given belongs to God and we are just stewards. Psalm 24:1 says, "The earth and everything in it, the world and its inhabitants, belong to the Lord;" It doesn't matter who you are, what you do for a living, or how much money you have earned; everything that you have belongs to God. We are just stewards. The stewardship idea is clearly stated in the creation mandate in Genesis 1:28 ("Be fruitful and multiply, and rule over." and Genesis 2:15 ("Cultivate and keep it'). We cultivate, keep and rule over the creation on behalf of the King of kings. Jesus's parable on talents in Mathew 24:14-30 illustrates the Biblical principle of stewardship powerfully.

Does God's blessing mean that we will always have material prosperity? Not necessarily. Psalm 73 answers the puzzle of "the prosperity of the wicked" (Psalm 73:3). The Psalmist says that this troubled him, till he came to the sanctuary of God, where he perceived their end. There, the puzzle was solved; he perceived their end. (Psalm 73:17).

Then what should be our attitude to money? Be grateful to God for what He has given and be a faithful steward. Matthew 6:21 says, "For where your treasure is, there your heart will also be." The problem comes not when you earn money, but when you start loving money more than God, more than your family and more than everything else. In 1 Timothy 6:10, Paul reminds us that "love of money is the root of all kinds of evil". The true test of our attitude to money is in the way we spend our money. Paul continues in verses 17 to 19, – (17) "Instruct those who are rich in this present world not to be conceited or to fix their hope on the uncertainty of riches, but on God, who richly supplies us with all things to enjoy. (18) Instruct them to do good, to be rich in good works, to be generous and ready to share, (19) storing up for themselves the treasure of a good foundation for the future, so that they may take hold of that which is life indeed."

The Bible teaches us about integrity and faithfulness. How faithful are we in handling the wealth that God has entrusted us with? In the context of Mary anointing Jesus's feet with expensive perfume, John tells us of Judas Iscariot in John 12:6, "Now he said this, not because he cared about the poor, but because he was a thief, and as he kept the money box, he used to steal from what was put into it." Even the person called to be one of the twelve disciples, not being faithful to what was entrusted to him. It is interesting to note the relationship between Judas's attitude towards money and his ultimate downfall.

Core Principles on Christian Giving (2 Cor. 9:6-9)[1]

One mark of the followers of Christ in the New Testament was their willingness to give their money to others. There are many models of gentile churches collecting money to help the churches in Judea when they were in need. Antioch church, Macedonian churches, and Corinthian churches all participated in giving generously and willingly.

2 Cor. 9:6-92 Corinthians 9:6-9

6- Now this I say, he who sows sparingly will also reap sparingly, and he who sows bountifully will also reap bountifully. 7- Each one must do just as he has purposed in his heart, not grudgingly or under compulsion, for God loves a cheerful giver. 8- And God is able to make all grace abound to you, so that always having all sufficiency in everything, you may have an abundance for every good deed as it is written,

"He scattered abroad, he gave to the poor,

His righteousness endures forever."

Look at the agricultural metaphor Paul is using here.

- Corinthian Church had made a generous commitment. Now he says, if you sow bountifully, you will reap bountifully (in some form) in your own lives. It does not mean that you will get material blessings in proportion to what you give.
- He plans to set aside the best of the produce, as seed is not used for consumption. Do we set aside our best for giving? How do we resist the temptation to use that for our consumption?

We have some guidelines here. Give what you purposed to give. All did not give 10% or the same amount, but each one gave what he had purposed in his heart. Our giving need not be limited to 10%. Their giving was to be cheerful, out of their desire to meet the need, not having second thoughts of their own needs. (v.7)

- We are part of a local church. We need to cheerfully purpose to set aside money to contribute to our local Church family and when needed for churches in other parts of the country and the world, for the progress of the gospel. —all with the view of contributing to the progress of the gospel.

There are several promises attached to giving. Sacrificial giving results in God's favor so that we will always have sufficient resources for our needs (not necessarily for all our wants). Remember that God's blessings are for 'good work' (Phil. 4:19 "And my God will supply all your needs according to His riches in glory in Christ Jesus."). Also, God's rewards are not necessarily material. The greatest blessing, we will receive, however, will come in eternity when we hear our Savior say, 'Well done, good and faithful servant!'

(Matt. 25:21). We will be rewarded beyond anything we can ever anticipate or comprehend while on earth. Remember the poor widow's offering in Luke 21:1-4.

---

[1] Some of the ideas here are taken from BILD First principles.

Christian Business Leader

Bobby was a Pastor and a business leader at the same time. He balanced these two roles very well. In this section, we will look at some principles of leading a business, which Bobby demonstrated as a business leader.

1. Work hard and diligently.

    The teaching on wealth is related to the teaching on work. Bobby believed in and practiced "working with own hands". He was very much involved in the business world. In Ephesians 2:10, we read "For we are His ***workmanship***, created in Christ Jesus for good works, which God prepared beforehand so that we would walk in them." Each of us is God's workmanship or masterpiece. There is a body of work for which each of us is created. Work is not just about doing a job. It is being engaged in something for which God has uniquely created us.

    The Bible teaches us that there are two key motivations for a disciplined lifestyle of work. We see these in Paul's letters to the Thessalonian church.
    - This disciplined work ethic will enable us to provide for our own needs, including our families' needs as well.
    - It will provide us with the provision for doing good deeds. In 2 Thess. 3:13, his teaching about work is followed by a call "Do not grow weary of doing good".

    We should not only avoid laziness and provide for our own needs, but out of the success of that labor, we should tirelessly do good before the watching world.

    The Christian work ethic that Bobby followed is stated in Col. 3:23-24 ^{23}Whatever you do, work at it with all your heart, as working for the Lord, not for human masters, ^{24} since you know that you will receive an inheritance from the Lord as a reward. It is the Lord Christ you are serving. Working with "all your heart" is at the core of the Christian work ethic.

2. Be an example by a disciplined lifestyle, as Paul urges the Thessalonian church. Business leaders and ministry leaders need to work hard and be an example for colleagues and everyone else we come across with. Paul urges both Timothy and Titus to set examples for others, in speech, in conduct, in life, and in purity, by showing integrity and seriousness. (1 Timothy 4:12 and Titus 2:7)

3. Personal and Family Financial discipline. Financial discipline begins in your personal life. Our financial stewardship is to be first demonstrated in the way we spend our money for personal and family needs and demonstrating our generosity. We need to save for our future, but we also need to have the right balance.

4. Accountability. We have referred to the parable of the talents already. As a business leader, one must be willing to be accountable for the structure that we have in the organization. Employees are accountable to the managers and the Accounts departments. Willingness to abide by the processes that the organization has put in place, being serious about all legal and statutory compliances, and paying taxes are all part of the accountability structure. If we are in senior leadership positions, structures such as auditors, Board, and shareholders are part of the accountability structure.

5. Employees. One litmus test for business leaders is how we treat our employees in financial matters. There is always the tension between profit and loss and employee welfare. How much is enough? In Colossians 4:1, the business leaders are called to grant the employees justice and fairness". (also Eph. 6:9). Deuteronomy

24:14-15 warns us against oppressing or taking undue advantage of the employees. We are urged to pay the wages on time.

6. Clients and Vendors. Clients and vendors (suppliers) are important stakeholders in the business. All the business income comes from the clients and a major part of the money is spent on suppliers. How we manage financial relationships is very important. As Christians in business, we need to be careful not to exploit the weakness of the clients – whether other institutions or individuals. So, having a standard rate structure based on the expected cost and reasonable profits is vital. Plan and pay taxes where it is due.

    Similarly, treating the suppliers as your partner goes a long way in the success of the business. Pay fair prices to them but remember that we have the right to insist on quality. Remember that they have their own costs. So, pay their dues on time, as much as possible. Treating our clients and suppliers with respect and justice will be a great testimony to the Lord.

7. Investors. The business leaders are also accountable to the investors, who have invested their wealth. They deserve to get reasonable returns on their investment. So, making a legitimate profit is necessary to sustain the business. It is also important to carefully plan how a business leader invests the profits. The returns or profit thus made enables the investors to invest in new business so that more jobs could be created. They will also be able to invest in creating assets that will ultimately help the business in the long term. More than that, if they are Christian investors, they will be able to invest in the Kingdom of God. So, it is important to practice financial prudence in reducing cost where it can be reduced and increasing profit, where it can be reduced.

Conclusion

I would also like Bobby encourage fellow believers and leaders to think of starting businesses where they can use the talents that God has given. Use the principles that Bobby taught us from the Bible.

I would like to close this chapter with a quote from John Stott, where he gives three options for a Christian who has been entrusted with money.

John Stott: [2]

"We have looked at the three options which confront all affluent Christians.

1. Should we become poor? No, not necessarily. Though doubtless Jesus Christ still calls some like the rich young ruler to a life of total voluntary poverty, it is not the vocation of all his disciples.
2. Then should we stay rich? No, this is not only unwise (because of the perils of conceit and materialism) but impossible (because we are to give generously, which will have the effect of reducing our wealth).
3. Instead of these two, we are to cultivate generosity on the one hand and simplicity with contentment on the other."

Dr. Babu Abraham

---

[2] John Stott, New Issues Facing Christians Today

DRAMA AND FILM:

Effective Weapons of Revival and Evangelism

By: Evang. Mike Bamiloye

We have come to the end times which, as the Bible had prophesied shall witness massive demonic manifestations and manipulations from the kingdom of hell. We have come to the time the Bible, in 2 Timothy 3:1 called: "the perilous times" and in 1 Timothy 4:1 moment of "falling away from the faith".

This is why there is such an upsurge in the demonstration and manipulation by demonic forces and principalities with the use of the channels of film and drama, as well as an unprecedented level of increase in the use of immoral dramatic presentations and movie productions that center on occultism, Satanism, immorality, and violence across Europe, America, Asia and the rest of the world. Spiritually sensitive adults can no longer watch many television programs and movies without changing channels to avoid insulting one's eyes with immoral actions. The hitherto simple and captivating children's dramas and films are no longer as pure and clean as we used to know them. In the past, children movies and programs on television were made to mold their hearts and minds into good moral characters, but not so any longer. Rather a good percentage of children's movies are now laced with subtle witchcraft and sorcery, violence, and immorality, making them unhealthy for the children's minds. Many times, you now have to sit down and watch many of these children's cartoons and movies with your children to give them the right education and morals from the distorted lessons of the animated movies. In addition, today, the emergence of computer technology has rapidly developed the use of drama and movies and even children's cartoons have now been upgraded to 3-D animation movies.

Since the release of **Harry Porter,** Hollywood has been capturing the minds of our youths and children with movies on witchcraft, sorcery, occultism and more captivating Halloween and demonic movies being made for kids and youths.

And what is the result of this demonic revival?

A young woman was once taken in a vision of hell and heaven. While in hell, she saw a lot of children being tortured by the devil, and she asked the Lord why. Many of them were possessed with rebellious spirit, hatred, disobedience, bitterness, and vengeance, through many of these animated cartoons and children's movies, the Lord told her.

- Children are getting more possessed with strange spirits of rebellion, stubbornness, and obstinacy.
- And youths are becoming more violent and disobedient to parents and leaders, and gangsterism and bullying are on the increase in our schools.

Consequently, the immoral impacts of Hollywood have destroyed the moral judgment of adults. This is mainly because many Hollywood movies meant for the elderly now are salted and sandwiched with practical violence, vengeance, and immorality The target and result of that is stubbornness against God, fractured homes with increasing divorce rates, rebellious children, infidelity, immorality and increased sense of independence from God.

Avoiding the Name of God:

Have you noticed that Hollywood is at the forefront of the crusade against the mentioning of the word God?

So, they substituted:

- "Oh Jesus!" with "Oh je-e-zz!"
- "For God's sake!" with "for crying out loud! Or "for Pete's sake"
- "Oh my God!" with "Omigosh!" or "Oh my goodness!"
- "Thank God!" with "Thank heavens!" Or "Thank goodness"

Thus, many movie producers have removed the words "God" or Jesus", from the dialogues in the movies; they mute the words from dialogue to show how strong their hatred of the names is.

Hollywood giving alternative names to sin:

They try to avoid biblical names for sin and unrighteousness, so they change the actual names to seemingly sweet, un-harmful names:

- Sex, fornication, and immorality is now known as fun among youths and adults.
- Divorce & separation is now known as incompatibility.
- Former husbands & wives are now known as ex-es.
- Girlfriend, boyfriend affairs is now known as mere dating.

Nollywood has been rated the 2nd largest movie industry in the world, marketing the same poisonous cakes to the hungry souls of the African people. Because of the hunger of people to feed on dramatic and cinematic substance, either sensible or not, they have embraced all Nollywood has to offer hook-bait-and-sinker. So, in many nations of Africa, by the representation of Nollywood movies, Nigerian people are wrongly known for voodoo, witchcraft, sorcery, and idolatry just the same way as Indians are wrongly believed to be dancers and singers, while Chinese are wrongly characterized as kung-fu and karate fighters. These are largely due to thematic and character portrayals in movies.

Drama is also extensively used for the promotion and marketing of businesses and products while governments and political leaders use drama for advocacy and national orientation and oftentimes to promote political, cultural, and socio-economic interests and values.

Generally, Satellite and Terrestrial TV Stations need entertainment programs like movies to shore up their ratings and thereby attract commercials and paid advertisements. The more viewers they have, the more adverts they attract to their channels. So, they maintain a regular flow of drama and movies to keep their viewers.

It is this gap that Mount Zion Films Productions and other Christian filmmakers have taken advantage of as an open door for spreading the gospel message. Evangelical movie makers send large volumes of movies to the stations without demanding money as compensation. This Strategy has worked to the glory of God and

Furtherance of the gospel. It is a common experience today that new satellite television channels now write to demand for movies, some for the take of their channels and some, to keep regular drama flow on screen. This underscores the value they place on drama and movies.

The role of drama has increasingly become relevant for a wide network of business, political, economic and cultural purposes, beyond its traditional relevance as a means of entertainment.

The End-Time Move of God with Evangelical Television Drama and Movies

All through the Bible, whenever the enemy was raging, the Lord always came up with a well-thought-out plan. When it seemed like Israel had no way of escaping from the ranting of Goliath, God was preparing His alternative, a backup plan. And David showed up. Similarly, God has a plan in place to frustrate the schemes of hell and the ranting of the devil that we have highlighted with regard to the immorality and demonic materials being churned out by the secular movie industry and mainstream media.

Whether Hollywood, Nollywood, Bollywood or the rest, God's backup plan for these end times is evident:

- He is raising up an army of drama ministers across the world.
- He is raising drama ministries and churches that will stamp their feet on the ground and raise the Lord's standard, projecting the glory and the virtues of God through drama and movies.
- He is raising up alternatives to the poisonous cakes the entertainment world is serving the world.
- He is raising up drama ministers and ministries in Nigeria, Ghana, Cameroon, Liberia, and other African nations.
- Beyond Africa, He is raising his drama army in America, Canada, Europe, and Asia.

Because the task is so enormous and the speed needed to outpace the Devil in this assignment is breathtaking, our God is using not only those who are called into drama ministry alone, he has also begun to use all available vessels and means. While God is using ministries, churches and congregations that release themselves to be among His end-time drama army, He is also using those who would surrender their gifts on the Lord's altar completely for the expansion of the His Kingdom and this end-time drama and movie revolution. Any person, ministry or Church that surrenders itself shall surely be anointed and enlisted in the Lord's Drama army.

To help speed up the revival, the Lord is touching the media houses to open for these movies all over the world.

- In Nigeria today, almost all Nigerian television stations have Christian movies in their library, which were given to them freely.
- Many satellite and cable television outfits in Nigeria and abroad are freely showing the movies supplied to them.
- Many drama ministries in Nigeria are pouring out on film locations and making movies that are becoming alternatives to the ungodly movies in the markets.

Seven Main Reasons Why the Church Of God Should Consider The Use Of Drama And Movies As A Formidable Weapon Of Evangelism And Revival At This End Time

1. Because we are in the audio-visual revolution, when political ideologies and principles, social philosophies, industrial objectives, and fake religious beliefs are now being dramatically demonstrated to catch people's attention. And the Church of God cannot take the backseat.
2. Because people are easily attracted to the dramatic presentation of ideas, doctrines and principles, the Church of God must begin to use what will easily attract people to listen to the gospel of Jesus Christ.
3. Because of the principal fact of vision which perpetually holds that what people see with their eyes stays longer in memory than what they merely hear with their ears. That is why one would readily remember a drama presented a long time ago rather than a recent sermon.
4. Because Church members and believers in general are seeking a healthy alternative to the prevailing secular drama and movies.
    i. Ecclesiastes 1:8
    All things are full of labor; man cannot express it. The eye is not satisfied with seeing, nor the ear filled with hearing.
    ii. Proverbs 27:20
    Hell, and destruction is never full; so, the eyes of man are never satisfied.
    Therefore, the Church of God must give the eyes and the ears a better alternative.
5. Because the devil is flooding the world with poisonous movies and the alternatives can only come from the Church of God. Only the godliness of the Church can serve as alternative to the ungodliness of the world.
6. Because entertainment is taking over the heart and soul of men, we must be ready to counter this attack with "**evangetainment**" productions, to rescue the soul of men from destructive entertainment.
7. And finally, because drama as a ministry has its root in the Bible and because the life and ministry of Jesus Christ was entirely an enactment of what is called: **"a drama of redemption"**

– **Rev. Mike Bamiloye**
Mount Zion Films Productions

God's call upon Women today and the need for our contribution to fulfill the Great Commission

– **Sis. Gita Surendranath**

Today we live in a world of rapid and radical change. Men's hearts are filled with fear, dread, frustration, and despair. Mankind has proven incapable of coping with the pressing problems of our time - the population explosion, environmental pollution, the rising tide of crime and violence, sexual abuse, alcoholism, drug addiction, abortion, pornography, urban sprawl, and widespread political, social, and moral decay. The answer for this sinsick, suffering humanity lies in the Power of the Gospel. This dark and desperate hour in the affairs of mankind is an hour of destiny, a time of unprecedented opportunity for Christians 'To Go' and share the Gospel.

This is the hour for which we were born to set in motion a mighty sweeping Spiritual revolution that will turn the tide and reveal to the world what the Glorious Gospel of our Lord Jesus Christ offers.

The Great Commission in Matthew 28:18-20 the command '**To Go**' is given by the Lord Jesus Christ to every believer regardless of gender. We all have a role to play.

However, the Jewish temple of Jesus' day emphasized male-female class distinctions in their religious practices. The literature of Jews, Greeks and Romans reveals a very negative attitude about women. It was a culture that considered women as inferior, mere 'human chattels' fit to be ill-treated. In such a social and religious context Jesus' treatment of women was 'Revolutionary and Striking'.

Jesus, by His teaching and actions, affirmed the worth and value of women as persons to be included within God's love and service. Jesus included many women in His ministry team like the Samaritan woman, Mary the mother of Jesus, Mary of Bethany, Joanna, Susanna, and Salome, not forgetting Mary Magdalene who was the first to declare the message of Resurrection. Jesus's inclusion of and ministry to and through women within his own life and teaching were a powerful witness to the early Church of the partnership of women and men in ministry.

In addition to all the above, the Redemptive work of Christ on the Cross of Calvary is of paramount importance as it broke down all of these partitions/ walls/ distinctions and every believer regardless of race, gender or other distinctions had equal access to God – Gal: 3:27-28. They were equal recipients of His Power, Grace, Mercy, Favour, Giftings and Calling.

As women, understanding our identity in Christ is vital as it gives us a purpose and a knowledge of our unique calling to share the Gospel. Apostle Paul in his letters also mentions several women like Chloe, Mary, Persis, Priscilla, Lydia and many others as co-workers with him in the gospel ministry.

God is the Creator, and His creative vision is big enough to include women from all walks of life, different backgrounds and cultures to be a part of building His Kingdom. His will is big enough to include young girls like Rhoda who commit themselves to prayer and virgins like Mary, the young mother of Jesus. His plans are big enough for women like Elizabeth, Rachel, and Hannah – all of whom experienced prolonged seasons of barrenness. His purposes include women with pagan pasts like Ruth, prostitutes like Rahab and rejected, adulteress women like the Samaritan woman at the well. He sees the marginalized and enslaved women like Hagar and old women like Prophetess Anna. God's purpose and plan include all women. He needs each one of us for His Kingdom purpose.

So, the question remains…………should women be involved in the Great Commission?

The answer is a resounding "YES "!!!!!

Some reasons why?

1. The Great Commission is the Lord's command to one and all. God wants all men to be saved……. 2 Peter 3: 9, 1 Timothy 2: 4.
2. God wants to reveal His glory even through women upon the earth……Habakkuk: 2: 14.

3. The task of fulfilling the Great Commission is enormous and it is imperative for women to be involved. It is important to know that two-thirds of bible believing Christians are women. According to Mt 9:37 – "The harvest truly is plenteous, but the laborers are few………". Therefore, it is necessary for women to arise and fulfill this great call.
4. Understand the enemy's attack against the gospel work. 1 Peter 5:8. Satan knows his time is short and so will do everything possible to hinder the work of God.
5. Ancient Battleground- Gen: 3:15- Satan's vicious attack on women has started from the garden of Eden. So also, we women need to arise in the strength of the Lord and resist him ……. our enemy!
6. The need to identify with our sisters, and our gender and to win them for Christ is both urgent and immense. See them before your eyes lost in sin and captivity. We women are called to set them free.
7. Last but not least, we all as individuals will have to stand before our Lord giving an account of our Time, Talents, and Treasure. Rom 14:12; 2 Cor 5:10.

In conclusion, I lay before you the greatest challenge ever given to mankind by the greatest Person who has ever lived on the earth. No matter how wealthy or poor, famous, or not, literate, or illiterate, powerful, or not you may be, you can never give yourself to any cause that can compare with this life-changing, even world-changing call of God.

This command of our Lord Jesus Christ to help take His message of love and forgiveness worldwide and to make disciples of all nations cannot be taken flippantly but we need to pay heed and go about our 'Father's business' with urgency for our TIME is running out!

Let every Bible Believing Woman 'Arise and Shine'. Arise as a Mary to birth spiritual children, as a Hannah to raise many Samuels, as a Deborah to give Godly counsels and lead from the front, as a Jael who with the nail of prayer and the hammer of the Word will kill the Siseras in the land. Arise as an Esther to go into the inner court in deep intercession to set people free from the hands of a wicked Haman. Arise as Ruth who followed her Naomi to glean and gather in the harvest for such a time as this. Arise and shine as a Dorcas who through her good works brought glory to God. Be a Martha and a Mary who opened their house for the Master. Arise and shine like Corrie Ten Boom, Joyce Meyer, Florence Nightingale, and Mother Teresa for the harvest is truly ready and the laborers are few. Arise and shine for your light has come and the glory of the Lord has risen upon you.

Let our motto be "My utmost for His Highest".

Sis. Gita Surendranath
Mission of Hope International

ROLE OF WOMEN IN MINISTRY

In the beginning, when God was in the business of restoring and reshaping the Earth which had become without form and void, God created man and woman in his image and likeness. God blessed them both together and said, "Be fruitful, and multiply, and replenish the earth, and subdue it: and have dominion over the fish of the sea, and over the fowl of the air, and over every living thing that moveth upon the earth." (Genesis 1:28)

While creating mankind, I believe God was making sure that this time He created and appointed a watchman to take care of his Earth so that history is not repeated. Also, God made sure that this 'watchman', who was called Adam was not alone in this job. The Bible says in Ecclesiastes 4: 9 10 "Two are better than one, because they have a good reward for their labour. For if they fall, the one will lift his fellow: but woe to him that is alone when he falleth; for he hath not another to help him up." So, God created a suitable helpmate for Adam who named her Eve.

God's initial plan was that both would function as a team. So, He made them equal, and gave both authority. But they disobeyed God and sin entered this beautiful Earth sabotaging the purpose of God and violating the divine order of God on earth. But praise be to God that the story didn't end there! Jesus, the second Adam came and restored what was lost including the authority which Adam lost due to sin and gave it back to His Church.

From the beginning of time, we see God calling and choosing people to fulfill His purposes on earth and women have often been an inseparable part of the plan. When God created Adam, Eve was a part of that creation. So, the woman was not an afterthought but existed in Adam during creation and we later read how God used a rib from Adam to create Eve.

Women have always played an important role throughout history in the advancement of the Kingdom of God. The Bible records how several women were used by God in different ways to fulfill God's purposes. I would like to highlight just a couple of them, especially those whom God chose to raise to a position of leadership which was completely against the norm of those times.

In the Pentateuch, we read about the leadership of Miriam along with her brothers Moses and Aaron. In the book of Judges, we see God raising Deborah and making her a judge over all Israel while all the other judges of that day were men. God chose Queen Esther and her position of authority to nullify the plan and purpose of the enemy who intended to annihilate the Jews.

In the 2nd Chapter of the book of Joel, verses 27 to 28 we find a prophecy that is quite familiar to everyone; "And it shall come to pass afterward, that I will pour out my spirit upon all flesh; and your sons and your daughters shall prophesy, your old men shall dream dreams, your young men shall see visions: And also upon the servants and the handmaids in those days will I pour out my spirit." The fulfillment of this prophecy is found in the book of Acts Chapter 2 when God pours out His Holy Spirit upon all the 120 disciples of Jesus who were praying, regardless of their gender.

In the New Testament, we find that the plan of salvation unfolds with the total surrender of a woman named Mary who said, "Behold the handmaid of the Lord; be it unto me according to thy word." And thus, she became instrumental in the birth of Jesus Christ into this world.

While closely studying the earthly ministry of Jesus, we find that Jesus always elevated the status of women. He talked openly with women in a culture where it wasn't appreciated or acceptable. Jesus had several women who were His followers. Again, this was against the tradition of those times. Jesus also entrusted women with responsibilities. He appeared to Mary Magdalene, and she had the privilege of sharing the good news of his resurrection with the rest of his disciples, thereby making her the first evangelist.

The Apostle Paul, like Jesus, had several women who supported him in ministry. Of the long list of people whom Paul greets in Romans Chapter 16, a good number of them are women. So, the importance of women in fulfilling the purposes of God is seen in Paul's ministry as well.

Jesus's inclusion of women among his disciples and witnesses, the coming of the Holy Spirit on both men and women and Paul's inclusion of women in his circle of co-workers in the ministry, all affirm the full and equal participation of both women and men in all aspects of ministries of the gospel.

The underlying biblical theology of a "new creation in Christ" in which there is "neither male nor female" is a powerful affirmation of the commitment to equality in the gospel, the Church, and all its ministries. Before God, men and women have equality in position or personhood. But, in the roles which God created them to fulfill, there is authority and submission which is carefully designed to preserve the unity of their relationship. Being under the guidance and blessings of the godly leadership placed over us, we have all the freedom to minister to God and serve God in whatever capacity God has given to us.

The Great Commission by Jesus was given to all His disciples, and it included women. Each person in the Body of Christ is required to step out of their comfort zone to preach the gospel to the ends of the earth beginning with their Jerusalem. All are required to be faithful in the call that God has placed over us. I know it's not easy but let me tell you it's not impossible either. Especially we as women, in our Indian culture and context will face many challenges. If we continue to persevere and not give up, we will succeed in making many disciples for Christ.

To be effective in our calling, God has blessed each member in the Body of Christ with at least one talent or a grace gift as mentioned in 1 Corinthians 12:7. And we are all required to put it to use and to multiply it. A day is coming when we will all be called to give an account of it. So, we first need to be recognized and understand the gifts and talents God has given us.

We can identify many ways in which women can be involved inside and outside the Church. One of the most important ministries in which almost all women can actively participate is prayer. We find many praying women in the Bible, who through their prayers turned around their situation for the better. Their prayers touched the heart of God and God was moved to act. An amazing woman who stands out in prayer is Anna in the gospel of Luke. She was praying for the salvation of Israel, and she was so committed that she did not depart from the temple but worshipped God with fasting and prayer night and day till she encountered the answer to her prayers.

God has blessed the Church with many other spiritual gifts and women should faithfully use the spiritual gifts which God has entrusted to them. In 1 Corinthians Chapter 11, we see that women can prophesy. We find prophetess like Miriam and Huldah in the Old Testament. A great awakening took place in the land during the time of Huldah because she fearlessly delivered the Word of the Lord for her times. Miriam was not only a prophetess but a worship leader too who led the women into a praise dance after crossing the Red Sea. Singing, leading in worship, songwriting are also ministries in which women can be involved .

Women may even teach. In fact, in Titus Chapter 2:4-5, the Bible commands the older women to teach the younger women. Women may also counsel others. I believe Priscilla, the missionary had both the gift of teaching and counseling. In Acts 18:26, we find Priscilla along with her husband Aquila instructing Apollos; thereby helping him to see the plan of God more accurately.

Women may testify and direct others to Christ. Like the nameless slave girl in 2 Kings Chapter 5, women can be instrumental in drawing people of influence to the true and the living God. Our effectiveness doesn't depend on how educated or knowledgeable we are. God can use us like the Samaritan woman to draw a whole village to Christ with maybe just a line of our testimony.

Women could serve the Body of Christ and even people outside the Church with the capabilities God has given them. For example, in Acts chapter 9, we read about Dorcas who made linen clothes and gave them to the poor. Through such acts of service, we can demonstrate the selfless love of God and influence souls for Christ. Like the Shunammite woman or Lydia, women could open their homes to accommodate and serve the servants of God in ministry.

Women could also be encouraged to be at the feet of Jesus like Mary to learn from him. For instance, when the Samaritan woman at the well conversed with Jesus, she was given a revelation about true worship, something that Jesus hadn't yet shared even with his disciples. In addition to that, her eyes were opened, and she had a revelation of the Messiah. God makes no distinction. Despite there being many religious leaders and teachers of the law, who were waiting for the coming of the Messiah, this woman who was despised and ignored by everyone received a powerful revelation of the Messiah. Something like that could happen to women who spend time conversing with Jesus.

Hospitality is another beautiful ministry women can be involved in, like Martha. Martha is usually quoted as a negative example in the incident when Jesus visited their home in Bethany. However, we should understand the context in which Jesus rebuked Martha. It was not for her hospitality that Jesus rebuked her, but because she was not doing it joyfully and instead, she was accusing and complaining to Jesus. Also, Jesus wanted to teach to prioritize listening to Him before other things. This should not lead anyone to underestimate the gift or ministry of hospitality.

Mothers too have a huge opportunity for an important ministry which is to raise their children to love and honour God, thus raising a generation who would stand for God. Hannah, Elizabeth and many other such women are great role models who reared their children to be mightily used in God's kingdom. We can impact an entire generation by the godly upbringing of our children.

Women may even take up leadership roles like Deborah if God has placed such a call upon them. It is not about grabbing or grasping a position but in due course of time, God will pave the way to those levels of responsibilities. In such case, the men should be supportive of their ministry. And when it is a man who is in the leading position, the women should support them in every way, through their words of encouragement and earnest prayers.

Women can also support ministries financially like some of the women mentioned in Luke Chapter 8:3 who were privileged to support Jesus's ministry. There are several other ways in which women can be involved in ministry. I have mentioned just a few.

In conclusion, I would like to remind you and mention some important things. First, you need to be convinced about God's call on your life. Secondly, in connection with your call, you need to be obedient to what the Lord is asking you to do. And you need to do that faithfully, joyfully, and fearlessly, even if it involves taking a risk. At the same time, you must submit to the spiritual authority God has placed over you no matter how they treat you. Thirdly, don't be in a hurry to make things happen. Be patient. Don't be a rebel. Wait for your time. God will lift you in due season. Fourthly, don't bother about the appreciation and rewards you may get on earth which will soon fade away. Fix your eyes on the eternal reward!

Also, do not try to imitate anyone. Be what God has called you to be. Finally, no matter how high you rise in Christian ministry, stay humble. The Bible says Pride goes before Destruction. So, train yourself to be humble. Also, never allow greed to come into you. Be happy and content with the lot God has given you.

I would like to conclude by repeating what the Bible says in Colossians 3:17, "And whatsoever ye do in word or deed, do all in the name of the Lord Jesus, giving thanks to God and the Father by him". Be faithful in the little God has entrusted you and He will entrust you with much. And when the Chief Shepherd appears, you will receive the crown of glory that will never fade away.

Sis. Persis John
All Nations House of Prayer (ANHOP)

Bobby Chellappan – In Memoriam | 1973-2021

– Dr. David Reeves

 Scan the QR code to watch Dr. Bobby tell his own story on Vimeo.n

In March 2020, Unfolding Word staff met with translators and organization leaders at the headquarters of our ministry partner, Bridge Connectivity Solutions, in Delhi. While there, we talked with the late Dr. Bobby Chellappan, who died in August of complications from a severe heart attack.

A much-sought-after ministry leader in India, Dr. Bobby left a successful career as a pastor and television evangelist to take on a new role: general manager for the Bible translation studio at New Delhi, a software company in Delhi. The following are excerpts from our conversation there:

We've been involved in the Gateway language strategy, which was started four years ago [in 2017]. The idea was to bring out a copyright-free, public-domain Gateway Language [text] which can be used as a source text for minority languages.

And over the last four years, we have been an instrument in developing these GL Bibles, which are now already in the public domain, called the India Revised Version. Plus, we are involved in developing resources for minority language translators, like the translation Words, the translation Notes and Translation Academy.

The Gateway Language Strategy is a very strategic way of approaching Bible translations. As we know, translations have been done in this country for many years, and it would take a lifetime for a person to complete one Bible. As the Bible translation agencies fraternity around the world have come together, there's a timetable for 2033. We plan to have these resources and the Bibles ready.

So, to process this and accelerate the work, we need a strategy. And Gateway Languages are one of the best strategies, we understand because as we develop the Gateway Language Bibles, in the minority languages, there are these bilingual speakers who know the Gateway Language and their language. It's easier and more comfortable for them to translate from a Gateway Language into a minority language, and I don't think it will ever work if we try to teach them the original languages. It's not practical. This would be the best approach.

We are so excited about this because of what we have achieved in the last four years in having the Gateway Language Bible under the CCBT process that we call Church-Centric Bible Translation and how the churches were involved in it.

It was not that we were doing this work. We are facilitators in bringing the Church community in that Gateway Language to come together and do the work.

It means that the Church now owns the Bible. So, it's not a Bible independent of the church. It's a Bible that has been produced by the Church from the Church of that language. So, they own that Bible and they are so excited about it.

Now, as the GLs are ready, there are about 738 languages in India. That's a huge work. As of now, we only have about 80 full Bibles in this country in 80 languages. So, that gives us a lot of work yet to be completed. Today we have technology to use, and if we can't do it today, then we wonder when we will.

So, the time is short, and things all around the country are not going the way [they] should be. There [are many] restrictions in the work of the church. The government is keeping a heavy hand on what is happening in the church. We believe that soon it will be stricter, tighter. This is the gap that we have right now, where we can push things and make it happen right now — in our times, in our generation. And I believe God is giving us this opportunity still.

Doors are still not closed in India. Still, the doors are open, and it's a time when the Church can come together and put all their force to move forward and get this work accomplished.

There are people, there are churches in all these languages. And we can use them to get this work done right now. They are ready and they are willing. And the churches need the Bible, like, yesterday. So, if we can channel all our resources and target this and get the work moving, we will have the Bible, as per the targets: Like, 2033, we will be able to reach that if we are really focused on doing this work right now.

I think to accomplish this, first, we must have a clear picture and a roadmap of how we need to move forward. Because sometimes I have seen that we move in one direction and suddenly, we just change the course and move in another direction. So, that will not help us go anywhere. We need to be focused as to how to do that. And emerging out of this GL plan, we should have a very strategic plan, like the Gateway Language, how to impact the minority languages. If we strategize this properly, plan it very clearly, and work as a team networking together, I think it can work in a much better way, not overlapping the work of what other people are doing, working together, and what is left behind, moving towards it to get the work completed. And those languages taken up as soon as possible and move forward.

Of course, in India, finance is a big problem. Funding is a big problem, because churches in these minority languages, many of them are new people, first-generation Christians, with no worldview of Christianity. They have no theological background. Many of the pastors have never had the opportunity to go to a seminary to study because they're not qualified to go to seminary. We need to help them, train them, equip them, so they can involve their churches and their teams to get the work done.

On the other hand, most often the Indian churches are from a very low economic background. So, it will be very difficult for them to raise funds to get the work done because they need to survive. And if there are? Resources that can help them sustain while they do this work will help the work to be completed in time and to be focused on it.

What is the imperative thing for India right now?

The whole idea of the Gateway Language strategy is that it's supposed to reach the minority language.

Now, if the GL is done — the Scriptures, and the Bibles, are made available in all the Gateway Languages today, which are on the CC by SA [license], in the public domain, and ready to be used — India would like to move forward and take up the minority languages. They're out there, and nobody's taking it up. We have the teams ready. The Church networks are ready. We have the tools, we have the equipment, we have the qualified consultants and the quality checkers.

It's very important to check the accuracy of work. What the original text intended must be correctly transferred to the minority language. So, alignment is what we are currently focused on, so that the Gateway Languages can be correctly aligned to the original languages and the minority languages can be aligned to the Gateway Languages. So, that focus is important. We are working on tools to get that fixed — very, very urgent. If this happens faster, then the checking process for the minority languages can be taken up as soon as possible.

I believe, as of now, the doors of India are still open, despite the persecutions. Churches are coming up everywhere. Even though the statistics may not declare it, in actuality, when you go to the field, you see that there are churches that never existed before. In almost all language groups, there are churches there. But they do not have the resources. The danger is that because they do not have Bibles or study materials, they are not equipped, strengthened and rooted. So, the danger is that at the places they came from, the backgrounds they came from, can easily divert them back and take them away. Secondly, wrong teachings can easily influence them, and they can deviate from the original calling in their lives. So, it's important to get the word of God to them and the resources. We can train disciples and equip them to be grounded, rooted and strong so that they can be kingdom builders and through them, the vast population needs to be touched. That's very important to be done right away.

In India, predominantly people are very religious by nature. But they do not know who the true God is. For us to reach them with the good news, Bibles are the key tools that can reach them. The literacy level in India is very low. And even though people may have gone to schools, they are not very comfortable with reading and writing. So, audio recordings would be very important for the Indian community. The Bibles can be audio recorded and given to the people in whatever channels or whatever way so they can hear it and be equipped and be strong. At the same time, India is a very closely-knit community. And if one person gets it, he will get it to the whole village.

That's the beauty of it. We're not a reserved community. We want to share things that we have. So, if one person has an audio or a Bible in their hand, he will go to the neighbor and share it with them, or the neighbor would want to know, what do you have? So, it's very important that we give them something which they can share or with which, can make other people inquisitive: What do you have with you? We need to hear it. We need to get the Bibles, the audios, and all the study resources, so the churches would be strong, and the gospel could be communicated effectively.

Dr. David Reeves
Unfolding Word
USA